CW01656269

HUDDERSFIELD
IN OLD PHOTOGRAPHS

HAZEL AND PHILIP TAYLOR, photographed by Wilf Cliffe in 1933, after a bluebell gathering expedition to Newhouse Wood.

HUDDERSFIELD

IN OLD PHOTOGRAPHS

COLLECTED BY

HAZEL WHEELER

Budding BOOKS

A Budding Book

First published in 1989 by Alan Sutton Publishing Limited

This edition published in 2000 by Budding Books,
an imprint of Sutton Publishing Limited
Phoenix Mill · Thrupp · Stroud · Gloucestershire GL5 2BU

Copyright © Hazel Wheeler, 1989

A catalogue record for this book is available from the British Library

ISBN 1-84015-178-1

Typesetting and origination by
Sutton Publishing Limited.
Printed and bound in England by
J.H. Haynes & Co. Ltd, Sparkford.

CONTENTS

INTRODUCTION

Uncle Alfred, who died in the First World War, was a keen photographer. Some of the local scenes he photographed were made into postcards to be sold for a halfpenny each in his father's Grocery and Drapery shop in Deighton. The name on them was J. Taylor – John being his father.

Alfred's huge camera, slides and other early photographic equipment remained untouched in the attic of Central Stores until the premises were sold in 1948. How proud Alfred would have been to know that, 70 years after his death, some of his photographs would be appearing in a book!

From an insignificant moorland village, Huddersfield developed into a leading manufacturing and industrial centre. Its cloth, engineering, musical and sporting achievements gaining world wide fame. William Ramsden (1558–1623) purchased the Manor of Huddersfield in 1599. The first baronet, Sir John Ramsden, obtained a charter from Charles II to hold 'one market in every week forever.' In 1681 Sir John gave a plot of land for a school in Northgate which was to be maintained by voluntary subscription.

The third baronet constructed Huddersfield's first waterworks in 1743, and in 1766 built a one storey building for 'the better accommodation of manufacturers and purchasers of cloth.' Almost the whole population was concerned with cloth weaving and on market days the Cloth Hall was a bustling centre. Merchants stayed overnight at the George Inn in the Market Place, three storeys high, with stabling and coach houses.

Canals were another factor in promoting trade for the town. Fifty years before incorporation of the borough, Huddersfield had only 10,000 inhabitants; but it was a busy centre for surrounding districts. Cloth made there was brought into town on market days.

In the early 1800s, Castlegate, or Low Green as it was then called, was one of the best residential parts of town. Anyone desiring to live there had to give a 'character reference supplied by his employer or clergyman.' Some of the best shops were in Kirkgate, many with horn lanterns lighted by candles at dusk. The tradesmen lived in the street, which was badly lit. Those who could afford it kept oil lamps burning over their front doors. Night watchmen, in sentry boxes, frequently dozed off. The peace of the town was kept by watchmen, who called out the hour as they patrolled the streets. They carried horn lanterns lit by candles – often obliging late night pedestrians who asked for a light for their pipes. The main streets, or 'gates' were Northgate, Westgate, Kirkgate and Castlegate.

In the early years of the last century a warehouse, in the middle of a garden, stood where the Town Hall is now. While on the site of the old Ramsden Street chapel there was a farm with a duck pond. On the site where the old Theatre Royal used to be, on Ramsden Street, great May fairs were held. Oh, that photography had been 'in go' then!

Travellers have always known they were nearly home when Castle Hill loomed into sight, the landmark which dominates the town. In 1829 18 Brigantian gold coins and 200 early Roman coins were discovered on Castle Hill. Its outstanding position made it the choice for the Chartists' meeting place in the nineteenth century and also for the weavers' strike in 1883, which lasted from 26 February until 5 May. Important events; jubilees, coronations, victories, have been celebrated there with bonfires and beacons. To celebrate the Allied victory, corporation workmen, under the supervision of Captain J.H. Irons, piled 40 tons of combustible material – mostly waste from local mills – into a bonfire. At 9.30 p.m. on Wednesday, 15 August 1945 the bonfire was lit by workmen touching the pile with torches. The flames reached as high as the Victoria Jubilee Tower.

On 8 May of that year a dance was held to celebrate victory in Europe in the Town Hall. So many wanted to attend, queues stretched outside for ages. Then there was impromptu dancing in the street – some played 'King William' outside the Ritz, and Free Frenchmen joined in the kissing! Perhaps it was as well that film was in short supply at that time . . .

Juvat impigros Deus Huddersfield's municipal motto, translated means 'God helps the diligent' or, 'God helps those who help themselves.' One citizen who carried out that motto was Betty Earnshaw, an employee of the old waterworks in the last century. She carried a large turnkey on her shoulder to turn on the water in various areas of the town, supplementing her earnings by fortune telling – one of the 'characters' of nineteenth-century Huddersfield. In 1827 Waterwork Commissioners improved on that arrangement by establishing the Longwood Reservoirs.

Huddersfield has produced some other notable personalities. Sir Walter Parratt – a fine organist, and chess player of such rare ability he could play without looking at the board. Once, he was challenged to play the organ and chess at the same time. The company adjourned to the Brunswick Street Methodist Church, where the chess board was set up behind Walter's back. A worthy opponent was brought in, and Sir Walter informed of every move. He began with Bach's Fugue in D Minor followed by others, all from memory, calling out his chess moves as required. He played beautifully, and won his game of chess.

Sir Harold Wilson, born at Cowlersley, was of similar resolute nature. He set his mind to become Prime Minister, although just an ordinary 'Huddersfield lad'. 'Getting there against all odds' could sum up the native Huddersfield character in such cases.

Another first, Huddersfield was the first municipality to construct, operate, and develop its own tramway system. Mitre Sports, formerly Benjamin Crook and Sons, football manufacturers founded in 1817, were then the second largest football factory in the world. The pioneers of British Dyestuffs were Reed Holliday, born in 1809, and Dan Dawson. In 1919 British Dyes became the British Dyestuffs Corporation – now ICI. Workmen toiling home from 'the dyes' in early years looked as though they were in a technicolour film, their hands and faces stained yellow. In 1853 Joseph Hopkinson patented the first compound safety valve for preventing boiler explosions, and Thomas Broadbent & Sons Ltd were among the largest makers of centrifugal machinery.

Southerners, although often scoffing at their northern counterparts, with their sooty industrial background of mills and grime nevertheless still drool over Huddersfield cloth. It is much sought after in Harrods – and you can't go better than that.

Workers made the most of their leisure time; singing in choirs and filling their lungs with moorland air on hikes into the beautiful neighbouring countryside. The inaugural meeting of the Glee and Madrigal Society, held on 10 April 1876, was preceded, Yorkshire fashion, by a 'substantial knife and fork tea'. The 'Mrs Sunderland' competition, which grew out of the diamond jubilee of the wedding of Mrs Sunderland – Yorkshire's Queen of Song – discovered many talented people, including Walter Widdop, the famous singer. For those with less cultured tastes, performing fleas were exposed to the curious gaze in a booth on Buxton Road.

In 1820, when the town's population was 13,000, an Act was passed for lighting, watching, and cleansing the town of Huddersfield. Housewives were directed to clean the footpath in front of their houses every Wednesday morning before 9 o'clock. They complied diligently, down on all fours, brushing and sweeping, scouring doorsteps and yellowing the corners with 'Donkey stone', a familiar sight up until the Second World War. So was seeing rear ends balancing on the outsides of sash windows, as housewives busily wash-leathered their bedroom windows, taking the opportunity to gossip with their neighbours – also hanging out of their windows – at the same time. (The forerunner of modern coffee mornings?) I wonder, if some passing cameraman had clicked his shutter, would they all have tumbled out, from sheer fright at being caught looking 'such a mess' with their curlers in?

Huddersfield In Old Photographs celebrates the lives of the many almost forgotten people who enjoyed the facilities of the town in years gone by. Just as, 'Music, when soft voices die, vibrates in the Memory' so do photographic likenesses re-awaken in us the triumphs and tribulations, and the example set before us by these Huddersfield people who influenced us in our youth.

SECTION ONE

Town

HUDDERSFIELD RAILWAY STATION, beloved by the late poet John Betjeman for its architectural beauty. Its foundation stone was laid by Earl Fitzwilliam on 9 October 1846. The frontage has a central projecting portico of eight Corinthian columns. Travellers emerging into St George's Square can see the comfortable George Hotel a few yards to the right. The station is now a listed building originally designed by J.P. Pritchett of York and it was built by Joseph Kaye of Huddersfield. The first public train ran from Cooper Bridge to Huddersfield on 3 August 1847.

A STEAM TRAIN ARRIVING AT THE STATION. Steam train enthusiasts now need to go to the Worth Valley to ride on one. Photographed in 1907.

THE TOWN HALL, opened in 1881, has been the scene of many splendid concerts given by Huddersfield Choral, male voice choirs, brass bands, youth orchestras, and on Greenhead High School Speech Days. Police concerts there have hosted singers of the calibre of Heddle Nash, Richard Tauber, Peter Dawson, Muriel Brunskill and Isobel Baillie. Arthur Askey performed his 'Busy Bee' song on stage to loud applause. Whitfields Johnson & Co., sold pianos, organs, harmoniums, violins, mandolines and banjos in Ramsden Street. The Huddersfield Examiner Office is situated a little further down Ramsden Street on the opposite side.

THE PEEL STATUE was unveiled on 3 June 1873. Lord Houghton performed the ceremony. A procession started from the armoury and church bells were rung all afternoon. Enterprising confectioners had erected stalls in Westgate, Chapel Hill and New Street. Heavily laden trains brought sightseers from neighbouring districts. Chief Constable Withers was marshall of the procession. Later, a banquet was enjoyed in the George Hotel, tickets 7*s*. 6*d*. each. Sir Robert Peel's statue, so long awaited, eroded with time and was finally removed in 1949.

ANOTHER VIEW OF THE TOWN HALL. Huddersfield's first mayor was Charles Henry Jones. 'Essentially a just and true man who stood aloof from the personal strivings often rife in municipal circles.' He refused to wear the gold chain presented by Sir J.W. Ramsden because he didn't like the treatment meted out to the tenantry by the lord of the manor, also because of his Puritan distaste of ostentatious display.

MARKET SQUARE. The Jubilee Fountain in the Market Place was given by Sir John William Ramsden on 12 June 1888. On the photograph the open top tramcar is passing Freeman, Hardy and Willis, established there in 1884. Hat manufacturer John Bagshaw was in business in the Market Place in 1845. Alfred Morton's Dining Rooms (to the left of the lamp-post) flourished there from the 1870s until the First World War. They were succeeded by John Hall's Dining Rooms (No. 7, Market Place). Lipton Ltd, Tea and Provision Dealers were in the Market Place from the 1890s, then Melia's Ltd. in the late twenties. George Hall, draper, had a prominent advertisement at the front of the tramcar – the photograph was taken in 1904. The Market Place is still a favourite meeting place for those wishing to simply 'stand and stare'. Ladies and gentlemen's 'conveniences' were installed in 1906.

RUSHWORTH'S CORNER, 'THE BAZAAR' at the time of the photograph in 1909. The shop was founded by Aquilla Rushworth in 1875 in the Market Place, before moving to the Westgate site. Until 1966 it was one of the town's foremost stores. In 1897 another shop, Ernest Barrett, Nos. 33–35 Northgate, sold cycling hose from 1*s*.6*d*. per pair, floor oilcloths from 2½ *d*. a yard, quilts from 2*s*. 11*d*. each, towels from 2½*d*., sheets from 1*s*. 11*d*. a pair. Also flowers, feathers, ribbons, laces, corsets and gloves. They had a fresh delivery of straw hats every week during summer. Also at that time G.F. Spurden, tailor to the aristocracy of Great Britain, No. 4 Victoria Lane, published extracts from satisfied customers' letters in local papers. From Thirsk – 'I am delighted with the coat and vest, it fits immense, and puts all in the shade over here.' From Manchester – 'I have a few friends here, and I can make it worth your while to come over and measure a few of us.' Oh, for those elegant days when the customer was always right and had never even heard of torn blue jeans . . . .

NEW STREET, the hub of Huddersfield's shopping centre. A Temperance Hotel used to be there, 'Centre of Light and Learning'. It was taken over by Joseph Thornton, a cloth finisher. In the coffee room he opened debates on political and religious topics, it was also popular for draughts and chess.

ANOTHER VIEW OF NEW STREET, in around 1907. The 'Boot and Shoe' was a highly esteemed resort. On the left of the photo, a sign for Marshall's pianos.

KING STREET, where in the nineteenth century the warehouse of Dunlop and Hastings, cloth merchants stood. Stumps of massive oak trees were found here deeply imbedded in the soil at the beginning of the last century, proof of the wooded character of the district in former days.

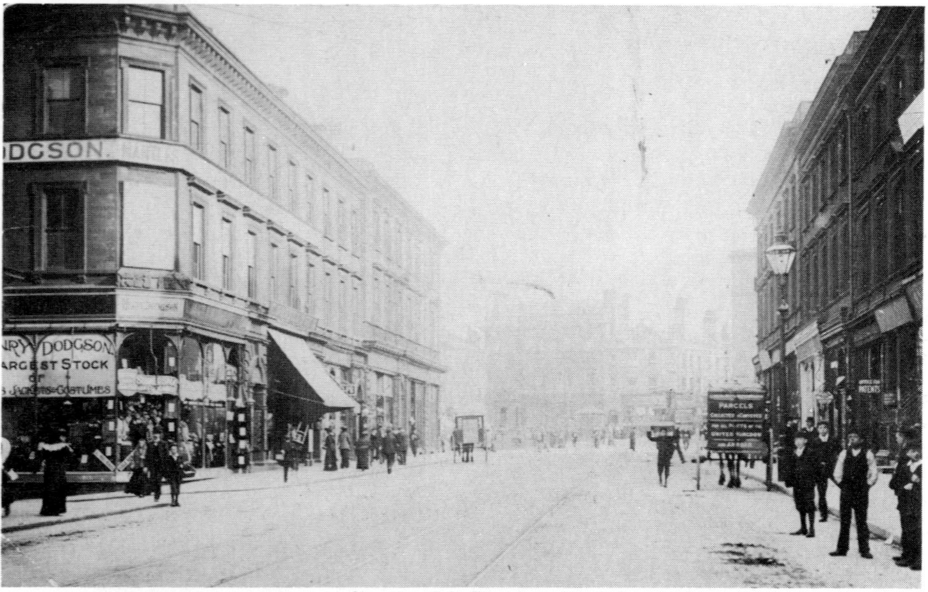

JOHN WILLIAM STREET was named after the 5th Baronet Sir John William Ramsden, born in 1831. Photographed in 1904, when Henry Dodgson's sold 'costumes' and 'mantles' for ladies. A summer sale was in progress. Note the boy with one leg and a crutch passing by, and on the opposite side a lad with a tray on his head, something seldom seen today.

THE LION ARCADE was opened in 1854, also the Model Lodging House. J.P. Pritchett of York designed the lion building. The famous lion of Coade stone was signed 'Seeley.' At one time it was supposed to roar at midnight, and once a crowd gathered in the Square as someone said it had moved! Ground floor shops in 1904 included George Jackson, tobacconist on the corner of Northumberland Street; Edwin Taylor, woollen manufacturer's agent; Harry Coulson Gledhill, hairdresser and Henry Hillman, florist. The Lion restaurant was run by Luke Waite. In the 1940s Mildred Dyson had a beautician's in the upper storey. The Huddersfield Building Society was to the right; the tallest building.

Bottom, right.
NEW STREET in the twenties and thirties was still populated largely by horses and carts, shop lads trundling carts and bowler hatted gentlemen, who always tipped their hats to ladies. School teacher Annie Whitworth, in sensible tweed coat and cloche hat, is caught by a 'Walking Pictures' street photographer.

ANOTHER VIEW OF KING STREET. Arthur Tabrum once prospered at No. 4. His motto, 'The Railway Companies will take you almost anywhere and at very low cost, and your pleasure will be greatly increased if you wear Tabrum's Easy Fitting Boots'. Cash prices 10*s*.6*d*., 12*s*.6*d*., and 15*s*. 9*d*. Joseph Benson, clogger and leather cutter was in business at No. 31 King Street. A slaughterhouse at the top of the street was demolished in 1807. Trams used to run down King Street on routes 1, 3 and 7.

GREENHEAD ROAD. Elegant stone houses at the 'posh' end of town where maids lived in the attics. In 1845 there were seven straw hat makers, two tallow chandlers, one truss and artificial limb maker, three teazel dealers and wood manufacturers, dozens of woollen cloth manufacturers and wool staplers in business. 'Ordinary' people would gaze at such houses in awe when having an outing to Greenhead Park. Employers, not employees, dwelt in Greenhead Road, Gledholt and Edgerton.

AN EARLY FIRE BRIGADE VEHICLE outside the fire station, in Princess Street. In 1898 the police ran the fire brigade.

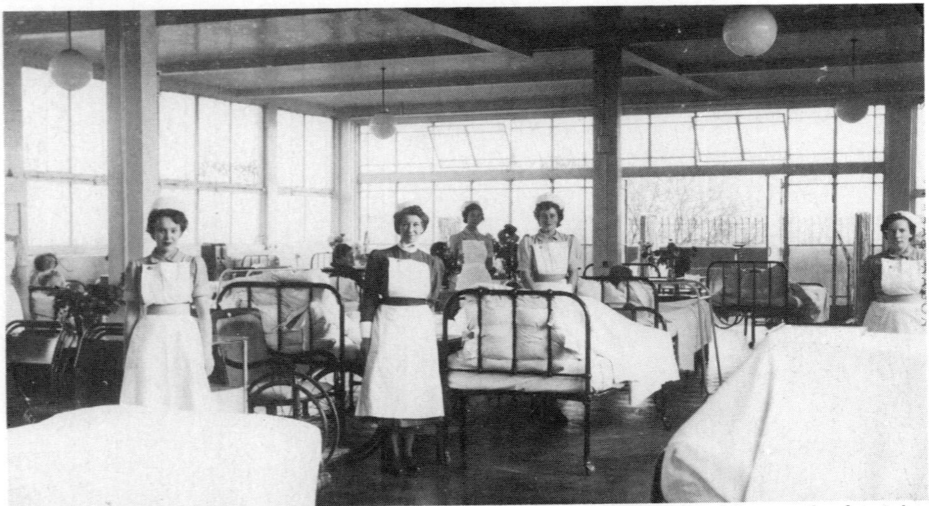

THE 'SUNSHINE WARD' of the old Royal Infirmary, 1954. Sister Lesley Venables, on the far right, when expecting her first child was made to wear her cloak when walking the corridors, and was removed from the men's ward to preserve decorum. State registered nurses earned £20 a month, living-in, probationers £4 a month. Sir Charles Ramsden laid the foundation stone in 1829. In the 1930s, West Riding Council Medical and Tuberculosis Clinic was in Peel Street, the T.B. sanatorium at Bradley Lane. Miss Isabella Smith was Matron at the Maternity Home in Greenhead Road. Private patients luxuriated in Green Lea, Acre Street, Lindley.

MISS HUDDERSFIELD AND MAIDS OF HONOUR, Infirmary Carnival, 1938. Daphne Broomhall, an 18 year-old shop assistant at Marks and Spencer's, was 'Miss Huddersfield'. A post office telephonist at Milnsbridge, blonde Mary Firth, right, and dark haired Ada Carter, a sweet shop manageress at Fartown, completed the trio. In the 1928 Infirmary Carnival, Denby Dale baked one of its mammoth pies to fund a cot for the Infirmary. The first resident medical officer at the Infirmary received £20 a year, the Matron a similar amount – with a bonus of £5 'if she had behaved herself'.

Above: OPEN AIR FRUIT, FLOWER, AND VEGETABLE STALLS outside the old Market Hall gates in the 1960s. Many housewives delayed their weekend food shopping on Saturdays until just before closing time; produce was sold off cheaply then. Below: The Dolls' Hospital and Porter's fish shop, either side of the old Market Hall, which was closed on 28 March 1970 and demolished in April of that year. Nine out of ten Huddersfield people who can remember, still prefer it. A staple food of Huddersfield citizens towards the close of the nineteenth century was polony. The Old Pork Emporium, No. 7 Market Walk, advertised 'Pork pies, sausages, and polony. Fresh daily, special Wholesale prices. Goods delivered to any part of the town or district.' Supermarkets don't offer that facility!

SECTION TWO

Districts

CASTLE HILL, Huddersfield's best known landmark, scene of archaeological digs and bonfires to celebrate royal and other occasions. In 1588 beacon fires were lit there on the defeat of the Spanish Armada. The first public house was built on Castle Hill between 1811–12, while on 1 April 1820 the beacon was set alight at the time of the Huddersfield Riots. Many Roman coins were found at Castle Hill in 1829. On 29 July 1863 there was a prize fight on the hill between Mills and Smith and a dog fight on 30 April 1865. The Jubilee Tower was opened to the public on 22 March 1899. On 14 November 1899 there was a fatal fall from the top of the Jubilee Tower. Just before the war in August 1939 excavations were carried out on Castle Hill by Mr. W. J. Varley MA FSA. On 15 June 1940 the tower was closed to the public and the toposcope (presented by Miss F.M. Clough in 1938) removed. People congregate on Good Friday morning there for outdoor worship and hymn singing.

NICHOLAS FENAY was the builder of the original Fenay Hall and was a governor of Aldmondbury Grammar School in 1609; He died in 1616. Records of the family go back as far as King John's reign. Jane Fenay, aged 23, was engaged to John Savile in 1713. On the eve of the wedding, 8 May, the bridegroom-to-be fell into a draw well near White Bear Inn, Wakefield. Both he and his would-be rescuer drowned when the rope snapped.

THIS CARD, showing the tiny post office at Fenay Bridge, was posted in September 1923. People in Huddersfield did not wait for invitations then. 'Dear Auntie' wrote Clara, 'mother and I are coming to see you on Wednesday for the day. Will be at your house about 10.45 a.m.' The card bore a red penny stamp.

CAROLINE WHEELER reflects on cruelties to animals – 'This is the remaining part of the old Aldmondbury Common. In this ground took place the last local bull baiting at the 1824 "Rush Bearing".' This was a triangular piece of ground where a bull used to be tethered to a stake with ropes about twenty yards long. Dogs were 'slipped' at the bull in succession. The poor victim was fanfared into town with a band of music on that last occasion. Many Aldmondbury cottagers kept bulldogs and it could be quite dangerous walking through the streets.

FINTHORPE, NEAR ALDMONDBURY. In 1937 Ina Hargreaves lived in Finthorpe Lodge, and a Mrs Mary Pollock also lived in cottages here in this pretty wooded area.

COLD ROYD HILL, KIRKHEATON, photographed in 1907. At the time of the hearth taxes there were 99 households in Kirkheaton and one mill, a third of the 99 were exempt from the tax because of poverty. The Dickin family who used to reside in the district, are said to have been related to Charles Dickens, the writer. Kirkheaton 'Rant' is the local name for the annual summer fair. The steam train was known as 'Burton Dick'.

LASCELLES HALL LANE, KIRKHEATON. The parish of Kirkheaton was much concerned in the Civil War, one minister being ejected for refusing to subscribe the Covenant. Another, of Presbyterian faith was in turn 'silenced' on the Reformation. The memorial tablet to the latter reads – 'Christopher Richardson, M.A. of Trin. Coll. Cam. and Lassell Hall, Rector of Kirkheaton 1646–1661 in which latter year he was silenced.' A window memorial in the church is to the memory of J.C. Broadbent JP of Lascelles Hall, a prosperous merchant, who evinced a warm sympathy with the industrial classes due to his efforts towards better social and economic conditions.

COMMON END, LASCELLES HALL. George Herbert Hirst, the cricketer, was employed as a wirer for a handloom weaver working in a corner cottage of a road that rises steeply towards Lascelles Hall. The typical sash windows on the photograph were the cause of many a trapped finger, and the outside 'privies' near frost-bite on wintry nights.

WATERLOO ROAD AND KIRKHEATON. There is a monument in Kirkheaton Church to commemorate 17 children who died in a 'raging fire' at a factory in Colne Bridge, on 14 February 1818. The overlooker, who probably lived in the mill yard, had gone home to bed, taking the precaution of locking the girls in. When fire broke out, the key of the door could not be found.

TRAM TERMINUS AT WATERLOO in 1916. The horse on the right is enjoying a drink from one of the water troughs provided for them. The completion of conversion of tramways to the electric system came in 1902. Huddersfield was lighted with gas for the first time in 1822.

FAR DEAN, KIRKBURTON. The tall chimney on the right-hand side of photograph was the building where Jeremiah Carter started a business in 1740, making hay spades and cobblers' knives. His descendant, Duncan Carter, still has a business in Kirkburton making miners' shovels and other implements.

BLEAK NAB HILL, DALTON, in the winter of 1906. The Enclosures Award of 1811 affected lands in Jagger Hill, Nab Hill Dalton, Dalton Green and Aldmonbury Bank. They were assigned to the Rector of Kirkheaton. Ardent Catholic, Richard Langley, who had a dwelling called Dives House at Dalton, was hanged, drawn and quartered for his religion at York in December 1586. He was beatified by Pope Leo XIII and declared Venerable on 15 December 1929 by Pope Pius XI.

RIVER COLNE AND DALTON BANK. The ancient town of 'Odersfelt' had its small beginnings by the confluence of two streams, the Colne and the Holme near King's Mill Lane. In the distance the former smallpox hospital can be seen.

A TRAMCAR wending its stately way up Trinity Street in 1931. The group of panama-hatted schoolgirls were probably pupils of Greenhead High School.

LIDGET STREET, LINDLEY. In 1899 Allen Gee, whose parents were handloom weavers at Lindley, began working on the staff of the Yorkshire Factory Times. He first worked as a piecer when only eleven, then a weaver at nineteen. Average earnings for weavers in 1891 ranged from 6*s*. to 16*s*. per week. Employment was irregular, yet it was said that 'princes were clad in cloth woven on the looms of Lindley.' Mr Gee was returned by the Lindley Ward to the Huddersfield Town Council, and by 1904 was elevated to the aldermanic bench. In 1907 he was made a Justice of the Peace.

NOTHING LIKE FRESH AIR TO BLOW THE COBWEBS AWAY. They dressed up in days gone by to trudge across Lindley moor! A brisk walk in such open country was certainly better than sleeping pills or tranquillizers. In wintertime walking warmed one up, and an overcoat thrown over the bedclothes helped keep our grandparents warm before the onset of such luxuries as duvets and central heating.

A HUDDERSFIELD CONSERVATIVE CLUB – Union Street perhaps? Those sloping tiled roofs, 'acks' children called them, were wonderful places on which to play. Caterpillars, on a bed of cabbage leaves in matchboxes were taken up onto them and raced by children. Matchsticks were frequently employed to give them a bit of encouragement at the rear ends. The caterpillar which undulated to the top of the ack first, won the prize for its owner – maybe an apple core, or a sticky toffee from the lad's trouser pocket.

MELTHAM CONVALESCENT HOME – Moor View, as it was known. Patients came here to fully recuperate before going home. In 1871 the home was opened through the generosity of Charles Brook. This is the hospital in which Harold Wilson spent three months as a typhoid patient when aged 14. Moor View closed in August 1968.

HOLMFIRTH ROAD, MELTHAM. David Brown Tractors' firm made its home at Meltham. Durker Roods, the family home, later became an hotel.

SLAITHWAITE, pronounced 'Slowit' by locals, in rolling wide open moorland. In the last century a glazier who lived there was nicknamed 'Putty'. He had a bad speech impediment, as well as a bad temper. One day on his rounds a tramp asked 'how many miles to Manchester?' Putty wanted to say twenty. While the tramp shivered and waited, Putty went on stuttering 'twe-twe-twe' but could get no further. Pointing the way, he blurted out – 'Go on, tha can be theer wol oi'm tellin' thi'. Slaithwaite Hall was once the abode of a knightly family. John Tyas lived there, in the most ancient structure in the Colne valley.

A BLEAK OUTPOST AT MOORESIDE EDGE for the North Regional Wireless Station. Proud owners of wireless sets used to take accumulators to be 'charged' weekly at wireless shops.

LAW TAYLOR WITH HIS WIFE, ANNIE, outside Elm Bank, Whitacre Street. (Note the obligatory aspidistra in the lace-curtained windows.) Many houses of this period had cellars where the washing was done with set pot, posser and mangle. Tin baths for bath night (usually a Friday) were also housed in the cellar.

WHITACRE STREET, DEIGHTON. Law Taylor, Mayor of Huddersfield 1924–6 lived at the top of the street. The street was tree lined on either side, and just round the corner to the left was the Sunday school. It was probably a Monday when the photograph was taken as washing was done on that day whatever the weather.

HENRY SYKES' CHEMIST'S SHOP, stood on this corner at Moldgreen. Lander's was another familiar chemist's name in the area. Their own make blackcurrant cough linctus sold at 1*s.* 3*d.* and 3*s.* Thornton and Kitchingman, Victoria Place, were slaters and plasterers, who whitewashed cellars. Ernest Drake, Ladies and Gentlemen's High Class Tailors, No. 271 Wakefield Road, Moldgreen, made 'Good enough suits for £5. Any man who wants to pay as high as £5 for a suit can have a fairly good one made for him at our shop. A few new pieces of cloth in are not quite up to the 1913 mark, but slightly better than last year's cloths.'

DOCTOR'S RESIDENCE, Storthes Hall Asylum, Kirkburton. According to the daughter of one lady who was there, patients in the 1920s had to work hard while there; washing, ironing, and cleaning, and her family had to pay for her to remain there. This must have been difficult on an ordinary mill worker's wage.

THIS MULTI-VIEW CHRISTMAS CARD of Kirkburton was posted to Miss Lodge, Whitehead Lane, Primrose Hill, Huddersfield, on 22 December 1906. Robert Lodge was a broker, frequently visiting Southport to bring furniture back to sell in his shop. The card shows the interior and exterior of Kirkburton Church, the old Vicarage, Hartley Lane, and another country lane in the locality. 'Wishing you a Merry Christmas and a Happy New Year, From J.S.' is written on the back.

SECTION THREE

Schools

THESE COMMEMORATIVE CARDS must have inspired a sense of pride and loyalty in their home town, when they were presented to each scholar in September 1918. The School Board, whose function it was to see that none of the rising generation grew up without an elementary education, came into existence early in 1871. Between 1874 and 1888 no fewer than sixteen schools were opened, with accommodation for 11,250 scholars. Huddersfield Board was one of the first in the country to introduce hand-work and manual instruction into all grades of school life.

DEIGHTON COUNCIL SCHOOL, photographed by Alfred Taylor. When the school bell rang, the girls had to line up on one side, boys on the other; infants went in by a separate entrance. Outside lavatories often froze up in wintertime, and one of the caretaker's tasks was to try to unfreeze them. He was always ready with bucket, mop and sawdust if a child 'had an accident', should he or she have put a hand up to ask 'Please teacher may I leave the room?' only to be told, 'wait till playtime'. In the thirties Oliver Smith was headmaster, other teachers were Alice Walker, Miss Wilkinson, Miss Charlesworth and Mr Goddard.

THE CHURCH SCHOOL, Chestnut Street, Sheepridge, also photographed by Alfred. Halfpenny postcards of the school were on sale in Alfred's father's grocery shop in Deighton.

THE FAVOURITE.

ON most of the great estates, and in many of the public parks, the Red Deer are to be seen, and form an attractive feature in the wooded landscape. In a wild state, in Great Britain, deer are only to be met with on Exmoor, where they are hunted, and in the great forests of Scotland, where they are also preserved for sporting purposes.

Huddersfield Education Committee.

Deighton Council School.

THIS CARD IS AWARDED TO

Annie Whitworth

FOR

PUNCTUAL AND REGULAR ATTENDANCE

During the School Quarter ended

Oct 31st 1905

J. D. Crosland

HEAD TEACHER.

HUDDERSFIELD EDUCATION COMMITTEE saw the wisdom of incentives to encourage scholars to be punctual and regular attenders. So cards, with coloured pictures on one side, were given to deserving children at the close of each school quarter. (After the same principle that cigarette cards were inserted in packets of cigarettes in earlier years, to encourage smokers.) Collecting is a fascinating and compulsive hobby – even worth being on time at school for!

AGAIN AT DEIGHTON SCHOOL Annie Whitworth, later to become a teacher herself, is seen here third from the right, standing. Seated, second left, is the future Mrs Alice Bailey. They obviously weren't asked to smile when having their photographs taken then – it might have been too flippant for such a serious business as school.

MOST LIKELY A PRE-FIRST WORLD WAR CLASS at Deighton Elementary School, as Alfred Castle Taylor is third from right in the front row.

LEPTON SCHOOL. An early village school, surrounded by fields. At last every child was taught how to read and write. In 1832, when a Huddersfield witness was giving evidence before a select committee of the House of Commons he said, 'When at the factory I had not any opportunity of learning to read and write, only a little on the Sabbath day. I do not think there is above one in a hundred in the factories that can write.' The use of child labour in the mills must have left the children too tired to take in the 'three R's' when they were at school only part time.

RASHCLIFFE C. OF E. SCHOOL PUPILS. How smartly turned out children had to be when at school in the early years of the century.

A WOODWORK CLASS at Huddersfield College. Surr Sam Whitworth, brother of Annie, second left on back row. Sam died of an ear infection aged twelve in 1898. What an unusual first name, Surr, and what a serious group of boys. Henry G. Barwood was headmaster in 1937 and into the war years.

NEWLY QUALIFIED SCHOOL TEACHER ANNIE WHITWORTH (first right) posing with colleagues. Huddersfield's first National School, situated at Seed Hill, was opened in 1819.

ALDMONDBURY GRAMMAR SCHOOL was given its charter and endowed by James I in 1609. Huddersfield boys who passed the Eleven Plus either went on to King James, as the college was also known, or Huddersfield Boys' College in New North Road.

HUDDERSFIELD TECHNICAL COLLEGE was opened in 1883 by the Duke of Somerset, and transferred to the Corporation in 1903. The educational institution from which the 'tech' sprang had its foundations laid by a modest body known as the Young Men's Mental Improvement Society.

ANOTHER VIEW OF ALDMONDBURY GRAMMAR SCHOOL. The Swimming teacher at Ramsden Street Baths in the thirties was Mrs A.E. Marflitt – who terrified those more of an academic bent!

HUDDERSFIELD BOYS COLLEGE was built in 1838, and taken over by the School Board in 1893. Philip Ahier, one of the masters, wrote *The Story of Castle Hill*, published by the Advertizer Press in 1946. Grey shorts, black blazers with badge, and black caps with the school 'house' badge were worn; long trousers were only allowed in the last year or so. Bulging satchels and gas mask containers were also features of college boys and girls in the Second World War years. If gas masks were forgotten, the offending pupil had to trail back home for it. Henry Herbert Asquith, Prime Minister, was a student of Huddersfield College. His mother was a Huddersfield woman.

ANNIE WHITWORTH, SCHOOL TEACHER wearing jet mourning beads. Annie's father died when she was a small child. Her mother took in washing and did other jobs to earn enough to allow her daughter to go to college – and was proud to do so. Mother and daughter lived in Barrow Buildings, Moldgreen. In later years Annie lived in Julian Street, then Belton Street. She attended Dalton St Paul's Chapel for many years.

A HEADMISTRESS OF STILE COMMON COUNCIL SCHOOL. Photographed by Thomas Dent of Burlington House. Teachers in the 1930s usually wore their hair done up in buns at the nape of the neck. It could be the trade mark of a vanished discipline, along with the unmade up faces and the ruler on the desk, ready to be administered to unruly scholars. In 1937 the headmistress was Hilda S. Brearley.

A GROUP OF ANNIE WHITWORTH'S PUPILS. She taught at Stile Common, Beaumont Street and Paddock during her teaching career. Photographed in the thirties, could it be a celebration of the 1937 coronation of George VI?

HUDDERSFIELD SCHOOLGIRLS CELEBRATING. The black patent ankle strap shoes look as though Cherry Blossom polish and 'elbow grease' had been liberally applied.

THE FOUNDATION STONE OF THE HIGH SCHOOL FOR GIRLS was laid by Alderman Willans on Thursday 27 February 1908, on the Greenhead site. Beneath it were laid copies of two local newspapers, a halfpenny, a threepenny piece, a shilling and a florin. The Borough Engineer, Mr K.F. Campbell, was the architect and the cost was estimated at £12,500. On 15 January 1909 the Huddersfield Municipal High School for Girls was opened by Lord Stanley of Alderney. The uniform consisted of navy blue tunics with velvet 'yoke', butcher type blue and white striped blouses and navy and blue striped ties. In the winter they wore navy hats, navy nap coats or gabardines, while straw hats with school hatband and navy and blue striped blazers were worn in the summer with the initials GHS on the badge.

GREENHEAD GYMNASIUM was also the assembly hall. In later years tunics were superseded by navy shorts and sky blue shirts for 'gym'. White dresses were worn for Speech Day in Huddersfield Town Hall. Tunics had to be no more than four inches from the ground when the wearer was kneeling. The school motto was 'Honour Before Honours'.

A GROUP OF GREENHEAD HIGH SCHOOL GIRLS playing netball on the field. Although hockey and tennis were also played, the emphasis was on academic pursuits. Both Greenhead junior and senior choirs were singers of distinction. Miss Edith Spikes was music mistress during the Second World War years.

A GROUP OF GREENHEAD MISTRESSES, centre, headmistress Miss B.A. Chambers MA (1909–18). This photograph was probably taken in 1910. Greenhead High School had to be closed in the summer and autumn of 1918 because of the influenza outbreak. In the autumn of 1939 school opening had to be delayed until air raid shelters had been built and completed on the hockey field.

HAZEL TAYLOR, PUPIL AT GREENHEAD HIGH SCHOOL during the Second World War years, when Miss Annie Hill MA was headmistress. Girls were forbidden to walk to school 'the college boys' way' under threat of detention. Boys were anathema! However, many risked it by cutting through Greenhead Park back to school after a tryst. 'Dig for Victory' allotments were keenly attended to in the school grounds. Uniforms could be bought second-hand in the school hall at certain times. They did not require clothing coupons, but lacked the bright newness of those bought from George Hall's or Kaye's drapers. Every item of clothing had to have Cash's name tapes bearing the pupil's name. What a long time it took sewing them all on!

ANOTHER GENERATION OF GREENHEAD HIGH SCHOOL GIRLS – Caroline Wheeler takes a look at her new school in 1967. Miss M. Owen was headmistress then, until 1971. Panama hats and velour winter ones had given way to navy berets with the school badge. In 1973 Caroline and others went on the schools' ship *Nevasa* for a Saharan Cruise. The cost of the rail journey to Southampton was £4.50 return. A postcard from Caroline that August related that 'they had to carry trays of food on the ship, and it was sliding all over. They looked like a deck load of drunkards'.

A NEW GIRL AT GREENHEAD HIGH SCHOOL, (centre) Caroline Wheeler, chatting with Janet Venables, left, and another friend on a seat outside Oaklands Home for the Elderly.

CAROLINE WHEELER wearing the once familiar Greenhead High School blazer of navy and blue stripes. In 1973 a man became headmaster, Mr G.L. Cooksey MA. Sadly, Greenhead High School for Girls in now a sixth form college, and only the memories and photographs remain of those 'girls only' years.

A GROUP OF GREENHEAD HIGH SCHOOL GIRLS IN 1971. Back row, left to right: –?–, Karen Edmonson, Josette Hall, Pamela Uttley, Judith ?, Julie Sykes, Jeanette ?, Janet ?, Eve ?, –?–. Front row, left to right: Irene Lindley, Carol Rodgers, Linda ?, – ? –, Miss Bowler (teacher), –?–, –?–, Wanda Ginty, Caroline Wheeler. 'Old Girls' will recall a verse of the school song:–

Above the turmoil of the breathless game,
Above the laughter and the song which never dies,
Above the quiet of unbroken work
Oh! let the cry of 'Honour' ever rise.
Refrain – Breeze of the field, gleam of the sun,
Well remembered faces and laurels hardly won
Will be with us till our working days are done.

PUPILS OF DEIGHTON COUNCIL SCHOOL in the thirties – now permitting themselves a smile in a few instances. Philip Taylor, third from left, back row; Kathleen Joyce, wearing a lace 'Peter Pan' collar, in the middle of row below. Third from right, seated, is Marie Clough; Mildred Horner, seated, third left, Marion Thomas, second left, seated. Derek Croft is on the front row, second right. Crossed legs and arms were the order of the day and hands on head in class until order, on the few occasions when it was lost, was restored.

ANOTHER THIRTIES GROUP OF DEIGHTON COUNCIL SCHOOL SCHOLARS. Martin Edmundson, back row boys, third left; next, Derek Hirst(?); centre, Leslie Moorhouse. Michael Bailey, third right; Donald White(?) second right. Dorothy Sutton, centre, standing, Marie Owen, fourth right; Seated; Irene Boyle, third left; Hazel Taylor, fourth left; Dorothy Beaumont, second right; Joan Potter at the end of row. Victor Law(?) first row on the right.

PROUD LADS OF PADDOCK COUNCIL SCHOOL with the football shield they won in 1938. Paddock School first opened in January 1881.

DALTON JUNIOR SCHOOL in the mid-sixties. Back row, far right, Richard Best. Second row second left, in striped dress, Jane Dalby; fifth left, Janet Venables. Third row, far right, Elizabeth Wheeler.

ANNIE WHITWORTH trying out her new Brownie box camera in 1921 prior to her trip to America on the S.S. *Montcalm*. The photograph was taken in the back garden (full of rhubarb) of Central Stores, Deighton. The Fields beyond stretched to Bradley Wood TB Sanatorium. In April, 1922, a No. 2 Brownie cost 13*s*.6*d*, leather carrying case 9*s*.6*d*., canvas case 5*s*. A Kodak N.C. Film (six exposures) No.120 cost 1*s*.3d.

TEACHERS OF STILE COMMON SCHOOL in 1949. Standing, far right, Annie Whitworth. Brooches were frequently worn to brighten up dresses in the aftermath of the war.

SECTION FOUR

Work

BUILDERS POSING to be photographed while constructing Central Stores, Deighton. Its foundations were dug deep, it took six months to complete. In 1903 John and Jane Taylor moved into their new home (the 'front' room was upstairs, over the shop) with a big living-room – kitchen behind the grocery and drapery store. There were mahogany counters and tiny wooden drawers to hold sticks of hard Spanish, twist, elastic, haberdashery. Huge bins housed loose flour and sugar, another Indian corn for the hens – all to be weighed out by hand.

JOHN TAYLOR,

Grocer and

Provision Merchant,

(my grandad

31, DEIGHTON ROAD,

HUDDERSFIELD.

Home-made Jams and Marmalade.

Prime Home-boiled Hams.

RASPBERRY JAM A SPECIALITY.

Agent for

Welch's Grape Juice

"Concordials,"

OR PURE FRUIT BEVERAGES.

"THE GREAT TEMPERANCE BEVERAGE."

Non-Alcoholic Invalid Port, Pint Bottles 1/6.

THIS ADVERTISEMENT appeared in Christ Church, Woodhouse magazine, in September 1901, price 1*d*.

JANE TAYLOR AND PUNCH during the early years of the century. Women used to buy shirts of the right size for their husbands by bringing a length of string, the measurement of his neck. Ladies' fleecy lined 'bloomers', combinations, vests, and best blouses could be bought for no more than 3*s*.6*d*. each. Jane was in charge of the drapery department. Back and front collar studs held those striped 'Union' working shirts' necklines together; clothes lines were hung on a nail, about 1*s*. each. Jane loved to blacklead the Yorkshire range until it gleamed, and the fire was stirred into a blaze with a pair of bellows.

JOE TAYLOR, just before, or at the beginning of the First World War. Photographed with the bentwood chair that customers used to sit on to 'get their puff back'. After college was over for the day, Joe sometimes helped in the grocery department of his parents' shop. Big tins of biscuits – Fox's, Huntley and Palmers', Crawfords', also needing to be weighed out, were in a sloping container in front of the shop counter. Customers often demanded 'a nibble' of each before deciding, as they did with the cheese.

ANNIE TAYLOR ADMIRING THE PLANTS in a Deighton greenhouse in the 1890s. In 1881 her grandfather, Abel Taylor, father of John, had a market gardening business in Deighton, continuing for many years. When Abel died, in September 1885, one of his sons, William 'Coddy' Taylor continued the business.

ANOTHER SNAP OF YOUNG GROCER JOE TAYLOR, among the rhubarb in the back garden. It used to grow profusely, helped on by being covered with butter tubs first. Rhubarb was sold in the shop very cheaply – a marvellous 'standby' for poorer customers. Starched, long white aprons were worn in the 1920s by Joe.

JANE TAYLOR, of Central Stores, Deighton. She and John lived in a 'low decker' before their grocery shop was built. They also had a stone outhouse where they made jam. As various fruits came into season the 'Jam factory' became a hive of industry. Village women were up at dawn to gather fruit and pile it into wooden trays. Helpers, in ankle length dresses and mob caps, sat on stools 'topping and tailing' gooseberries and emptying bits into the ashpit outside. Hymns were sung as they worked round the big earthenware bowl.

JOHN TAYLOR, proprietor, Central Stores, 168 Deighton Road. Photographed by H. Kruger, Artist and Photographer, of Northumberland Street, Huddersfield, and Bridge Street, Slaithwaite. As a young man working for a grocer in Huddersfield, he was sacked through no fault of his own. With a wife and young baby to provide for John bought a pound of best butter, placed it on a table in the front window of their 'low decker' for Jane to sell, while he went to customers of the Huddersfield grocer asking for their patronage if he started in business on his own accord. He was so well respected that he was soon able to make plans for building his own shop.

JOE TAYLOR OUTSIDE CENTRAL STORES, Deighton, in the 1930s. Khaki smock, flat cap (to lessen the impact of carrying trays of bread in from the bakehouse?) and pencil behind the ear – *de rigeur* outfit for the working day. By this time chocolate and cigarette machines had been installed outside the shop, and later a sign 'You May Telephone From Here'. Children played 'Puss, Puss, Come to my Corner' on the shop square when the gas lamp was lit.

AN EARLY HUDDERSFIELD FIRE BRIGADE VEHICLE. Standing, second left, Enoch Hutton, uncle of famous cricketer Len. From 1868–79 the fire brigade consisted of volunteer firemen only. The only fire appliances were two hose carts, one horse-drawn fire engine, and a fire escape. Horses were supplied by a local cab proprietor in case of fire. The only means of notifying the firemen was by blowing a fog horn at the main entrance in Princess Street.

ENOCH HUTTON AND HUDDERSFIELD GIRL GUIDES enjoying fire drill practice. In 1895 David Brown's engineering works was destroyed by fire.

EARLY HUDDERSFIELD FIRE ENGINE, driven by Enoch Hutton with some boy scouts.

EAGER HUDDERSFIELD SCHOOLBOYS learning fire drill from Enoch Hutton probably in the twenties or early thirties.

A WORKING MAN in the early half of the century, taking life easy for a change, resting on one of the dry stone walls in Huddersfield district. On the back of the photograph Annie Whitworth has written 'Uncle Law'. (Law Whitworth, not to be confused with Law Taylor.)

TYPICAL HUDDERSFIELD 'WORKING MEN' in the early years of the century. Some were market gardeners. They sometimes had contests among themselves – such as who could produce the longest piece of grass – just for a bit of fun. Most working men in and around Huddersfield lived in rented houses then. Life was hard, but food produced in their gardens was wholesome and pure.

THIS PHOTOGRAPH WAS DELIBERATELY MUTILATED by Lancelot Luxton Herbert Coldwell Key – who cut off his father's image after a row with him. 'Lance' was christened after four blind piano tuners. The Key household worked to the ticking of many and varied clocks, including grandfather and grandmother clocks. Betty, now Mrs Norman Swales, daughter of Lance, continued the musical tradition of the family. She played the cello with Lindley Brass Band, and at Huddersfield Theatre Royal.

F.C. KEY, PIANOS, of No. 109 Bradford Road, at the Huddersfield Trades' Exhibition. 'The House of Keys is The House to Please' sign was always displayed in the shop windows.

EARLY ADVERTISING BY HORSE AND CART. 'Wilson's Gas Cookers on Hire.' 'Coal is Dear, Gas is Cheap.' Another form of advertising was on big tin signs outside shops; 'Bisto Kids' with noses in the air, 'Colman's Mustard', 'Players Please'. This photograph was advertising an exhibit of the Kirkburton Gas Light Company. Also on the waggon are advertised Luton Cocoa, CWS 'Laundry Belle' made at Irlam, CWS Soap and Candle Works, Irlam, and CWS English Dessert Fruits.

A LOCAL ABATTOIR IN 1908. The Huddersfield cattle market and fairground was opened in 1881. In 1931 the Great Yorkshire Agricultural Show was held in Huddersfield.

HUDDERSFIELD BUS CREW on the Uppermill, Marsden route in the 1920s or early '30s. The first car run to Lockwood was on 6 November 1882. Visitors coming to the town for shopping or recreation naturally increased with the growth of motor services. Passengers carried on corporation buses between Holmebridge and Huddersfield on 25 August 1925 numbered 5,158. On the same date in 1928 the number had increased to 7,684.

SYDNEY GREGORY AND A COLLEAGUE HARD AT WORK. In early working life Syd worked for Benjamin Crook, in the twenties the second largest football factory in the world (now Mitre Sports). Crook's was founded in 1817. Syd also worked for Morley Brothers, Sheet Metal Works and David Brown Tractors, Meltham.

BEEVERS, UNIFORM MAKERS OF MOLDGREEN had a challenging task which was successfully accomplished some years ago. They had to first measure up, then make uniforms for chimpanzees of a circus. The premises in Wakefield Road are now named Ronald Gill, Tailor. In 1909 Beevers of Brook Street boasted the 'finest coloured catalogue of Military and Band Uniforms, containing 50 coloured figures in full uniform and over 200 other illustrations, in book form, post free, 2*s.* 6*d*.'

EMPLOYEES OF GOLCAR CO-OP ready to go on their annual trip. Hanson's were the bus company chosen to take them. Roy Firth, for many years the conductor of Honley Male Voice Choir, is second left on the front row.

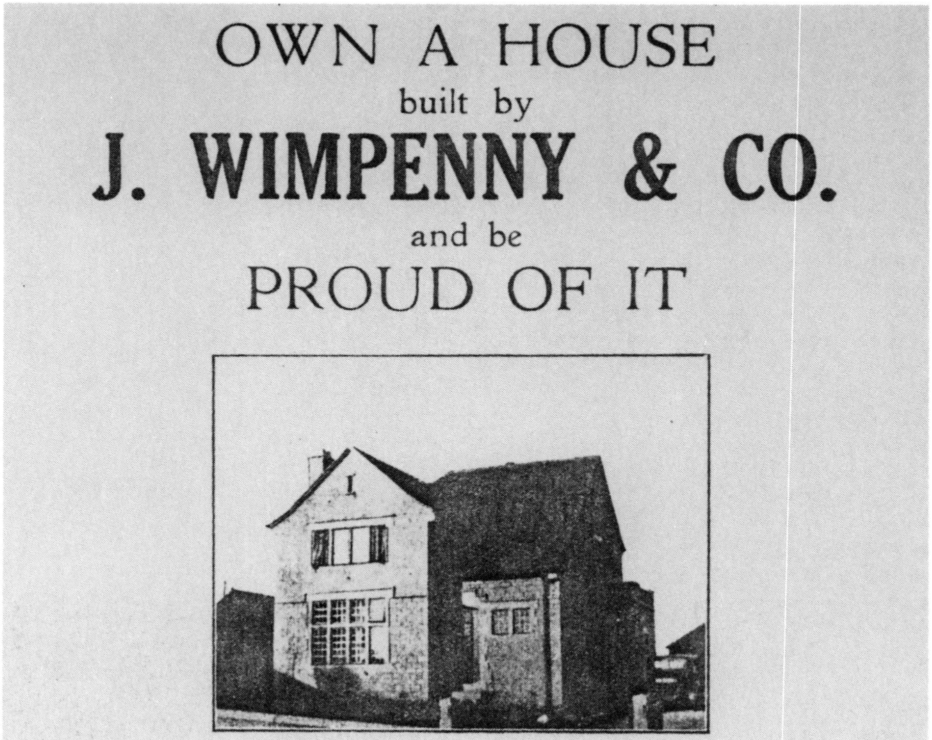

WIMPENNY, OF LINTHWAITE, is a well-known firm of builders. These house prices applied in 1935. During the same period Isaac Timmins Ltd, advertised houses on the Greenhead Estate, Dalton, from £395 upwards. While R. Smith of 76 Luck Lane, Marsh, built houses from £420, a small deposit was required with repayments of 10*s*. 6*d*. per week.

SECTION FIVE

Sport

THE FAMED HUDDERSFIELD TOWN TEAM. Schoolchildren could recite their surnames off by heart, they idolized them, chasing them for autographs at matches, but never becoming nuisances. It used to be a pleasure to stand on the terrace and watch football matches prior to modern times; the camaradie was wonderful, even between opposing teams and their supporters.

AN EARLY CRICKET TEAM. George Harold Brummit wearing dark waistcoat and pads.

ASPIRING DEIGHTON SCHOOLBOY FOOTBALLERS. Photographed at the recreation ground behind the Woolpack public house, just before the outbreak of the First World War. Brothers Joe Taylor and Alfred are seated, second and third left.

JACK FIRTH in the 1940s, a prominent Huddersfield billiard player. Living at Deighton then, Jack now lives at Netherton and is still enjoying the game.

ALL ENGLAND BILLIARD CHAMPION, VICTOR MUFF, second left, Jack Firth, second right and P. Clelland, far right. Also in the photograph are C. Delamare, T. Cawthrey and R. Taylor. In the mid-1940s the WMC League Cup was won by the Dyers' and Finishers' snooker and billiard team. The individual cups were both won by Jack Firth.

DEIGHTON YMCA FOOTBALL HOPEFULS Under 18 Team. Including: left, kneeling, Roy Medley; Jackie Palmer; Alan Scott. John Babb; Back row, second left, Philip Taylor; Donald Poppleton and Ralph Carter, far right.

ANOTHER GROUP OF DEIGHTON YMCA LADS. Standing, far right Leslie Moorhouse, far left, Philip Taylor next to Donald Poppleton. Far right, kneeling, John Babb, Alan Scott, Tommy Bainbridge in dark jumper. Frank McEvoy to the right of Tommy. Donald McEvoy later played for Huddersfield Town. The lads used to train on Leeds Road playing fields.

HUDDERSFIELD GOLF CLUB in a tranquil setting. The town can lay claim to initiating county golf. At the instigation of Dr Mackenzie, Mr A.L. Woodhead called a meeting of representatives of Yorkshire clubs. The outcome being the formation of the Yorkshire Union of Golf Clubs. In the early years the greatest golfer in the district was H.H. Barker, who also won the Irish Open Championship against a strong field. Huddersfield has a number of golf clubs, all in pleasant surroundings – Outlane, Woodsome, Longley.

WHITTAKER'S RIDING SCHOOL AT OUTLANE, home of John Whittaker, famous show jumper and rider. A first riding lesson in 1966 with Mrs. Whittaker leading the horses.

SHAW BROTHERS OF ASPLEY, SOCIAL AND BOWLING CLUB TEAM. On the trip to Bridlington in 1959, Granville Wheeler is on the back row, left. Wagon driver Johnny Egan, to the right of the bus at the back. Also on the photograph are Lewis Shaw, warehouseman, and Kenneth Shaw, designer.

FRED LUNN, FORMER HUDDERSFIELD TOWN FOOTBALLER, outside the White Horse Inn, Leeds Road, where he was landlord for a number of years. Fred was a life-long teetotaller who took up golfing in retirement. He played at Longley, then Outlane, finally at Bare, Morecambe, where he and his wife Ella spent their last years.

SECTION SIX

Wartime Huddersfield

ALFRED CASTLE TAYLOR, as a soldier in the First World War. 'I Vow To Thee, My Country, All Earthly Things Above' was proudly adhered to by the young men who rushed to defend England.

GOING FOR A WALK was one of the few pleasures left during the First World War. At least there were still plenty of wide open spaces, fields and woods in and around Huddersfield. Annie Whitworth, seen here with her cousin Alfred Taylor, gathered nettles on such excursions to make into soup. Gathering blackberries to bottle or make into pies was another pleasant pastime in autumn. This photograph was taken in 1915 in fields near Bradley Wood.

STANDING 'AT EASE' – Punch, the shop dog, included. Alfred Taylor, with a soldier friend, and Punch. Alfred died of meningitis at Rugeley Camp, Staffordshire in 1918. When John, his father, went to visit him that bitterly cold January day, Alfred had some cigarette packets on his bed. He was delirious, and thought he was serving in the shop, at home. 'Tell Joe to be a good boy' were his last words.

SYDNEY GREGORY, OF COWLERSLEY, a member of the Home Guard during the Second World War. On duty in the blackout up by Crosland Moor quarries, he missed his way one night and fell into a quarry. He wasn't found until next day. It could be almost as dangerous in Huddersfield when the blackout was in force as being 'in the front line'. The number of times accidents, due to bumping into lamp-posts, was reported in the *Examiner*! A well-known ARP post was at the Warrenfield Hotel, Sheepridge.

MRS ROBERT HENDERSON, then of No. 45, Glenfield Avenue, Deighton, with one of her soldier sons. One of the worries in the district during the Second World War was that 'Jerry' would drop a bomb on ICI. Fortunately they never did. In 1940, however, there was an air raid in the vicinity of Castle Hill, when on 29 August, German aeroplanes dropped bombs at Hall Bower.

ERNIE HAIGH HOME ON LEAVE, at a family reunion. Winifred Halstead, kneeling, daughter Carol wearing one of the knitted 'Pixie Hoods' so popular at the time. Brian Halstead in regulation school gabardine and cap, Philip Taylor kneeling, next to 'Wyn'. Mrs Halstead senior, is on the back row wearing a fur coat. Ernie was blown up in a tank, and never found. He wrote a diary of army life describing the scenes at Dunkirk.

A WHOLE NEW VARIETY OF DANCE PARTNERS was available during the Second World War, Polish, Belgian, the occasional Free French man, GI's with their gifts of nylons and 'gum'. Here is Hazel Taylor, photographed at Dumont studio with Belgian soldier Louis Dettier in 1945.

MURIEL HAIGH, then a member of Huddersfield Choral and Amateur Dramatic Societies as well as lead singer in Jackson Bridge Methodist productions. When a stewardess at the Royal Naval College, Greenwich in 1942, she had an opportunity to sing on the wireless. Brother Douglas, serving in West Africa, was 'listening in' when suddenly he heard a familiar voice singing from *Madame Butterfly*. 'That's my sister!' he yelled with delight. The programme was *Merry Go Round*.

AUDREY CUDWORTH OF BRADLEY BAR, on war work at GEC, Bailiff Bridge. A bank employee at National Provincial, Westgate, in 'Civvy Street'.

HUDDERSFIELD BOYS RUSHED TO JOIN THE ATC in the hope that one day, when they were old enough, they would fly Spitfires and Hurricanes. Here is Philip Taylor in the airforce blue uniform of the Air Training Corps.

JUNE HARRIS, left, of Sheepridge, and Hazel Taylor. June joined the WAAF, and was stationed in Padgate. Both girls were regular patrons of dances at the Town Hall and Cambridge Road Baths. Last buses to outlying districts left early during the war. If they were full, dancers simply had to walk home in the blackout. Quite fun if a few teamed up together! June is wearing a jigger coat in the photograph.

Chapels, Churches, Sunday Schools

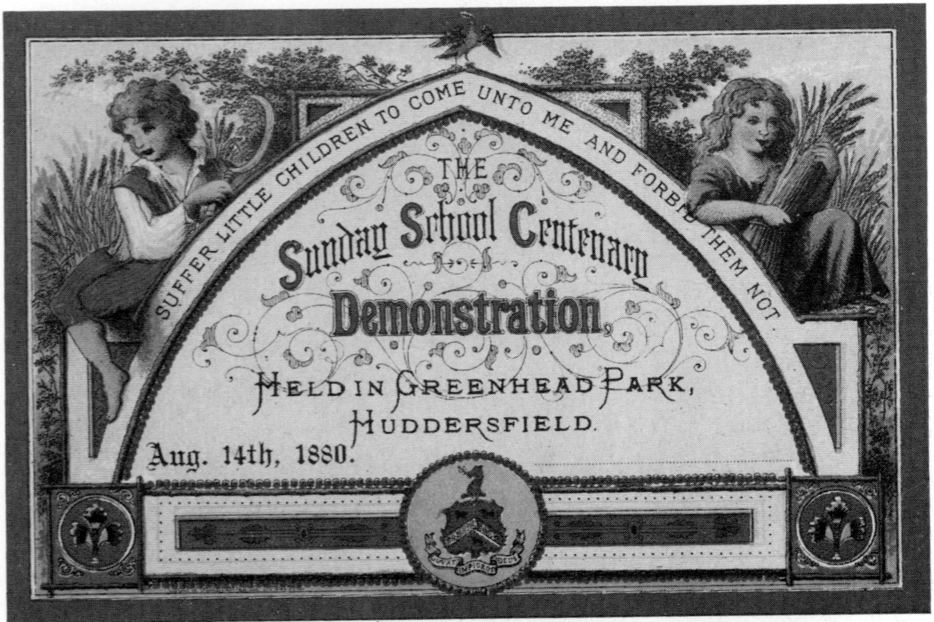

SUNDAY SCHOOL CENTENARY 1880. The mills closed at twelve. A banner of white calico followed the Mayor's procession, then members of 67 Sunday schools accompanied by Meltham Mills Band, Huddersfield Rifles and others. Flags carried the names of the schools, waggons were decorated with evergreens, scroll work and flowers. Workhouse children were also in the procession. *En route*, cans of water were handed to the little ones who were suffering from dust and heat. Waggons and horses were judged in Rifle Field. Newsome MFC school won first prize, 25*s*. The best pair of groomed horses were from Netheroyd Hill, Pickford & Co. Carriers were second, winning 15*s*. The procession totalled 20,000 – 'their appearance bore the strongest testimony to the beneficial effects of Sunday School training, in calling forth right influences in the minds of the young.' A roll on the drums called for attention before the hymn singing, which included 'Here with our United Voices', 'Hosanna! be the Children's Song', and 'From all that dwell below the Skies' to tune Old Hundredth. Many were too fatigued to sing. After tea (costing 1*s*.) bands played, children danced round a maypole or watched a Punch and Judy show. After 18,500 medals were distributed to the children, the centenary closed with a firework display.

PARISH CHURCH. In around 1100 the first Huddersfield Parish Church was built, in 1506 the second, the third was opened in 1832. Many 'grave and learned divines' have held the vicariate one memorable encumbant, the Revd Henry Venn MA, ministered for 12 years between 1759–71. He was associated with John Wesley, who preached in the parish church a number of times. Venn was the author of *The Complete Duty of Man*.

ALDMONDBURY PARISH CHURCH AND WAR MEMORIAL. Originally, Aldmondbury was of more importance than Huddersfield. Its church was erected in 1522. Wormald's building, a picturesque half-timbered house opposite the church, is now a Conservative club. Mention was made of Huddersfield in the Domesday Book, but its growth took place in the eighteenth and nineteenth centuries.

SOUTH CROSLAND CHURCH, by the quarries. In 1778 it was decreed that each churchwarden was to have a pint of community wine for his own use on Easter Sunday.

KIRKHEATON CHURCH. The discovery of a Saxon tombstone with runic inscription fortified the tradition that the early church was founded by missionaries of Paulinus in the seventh century. The area originally within the spiritual jurisdiction of Kirkheaton was extensive, then Denby Grange was added to the parish of Flockton and Houses Hill district, both formerly in the ancient parish of Kirkheaton. In the Beaumont Chapel reposed the recumbant figure of Richard Beaumont, widely known in early years as 'Black Dick'.

ARMITAGE BRIDGE CHURCH was burnt down in 1987 and then later rebuilt. In 1759, John Wesley, on his first visit to Huddersfield and district, wrote 'I rode over the mountains to Huddersfield, a wilder people I never saw in England.' Another time, preaching in the locality, 'The wildest congregation I have seen in Yorkshire – yet they were restrained by an unseen hand, and I believe some felt the sharpness of his word.' The first Wesleyan Society was formed at Netherthong.

MILTON CHURCH was opened on 18 June 1885. The photograph shows a decorated float to celebrate Whit Tuesday, 1912. Band of Hope meetings were very strongly supported. At the meeting in Milton Church on 24 October 1900, there was a piano solo by Miss Annie Raynor and a reading by Miss Clara Thomas. The following month saw recitations by Misses Martha and Liza Paxman, and a solo by the chairman. An excellent address was delivered by Mr J. Stocks on 'Why we should be teetotal'. Milton Church Clothing Club began in 1899 formed with a view of fostering habits of thrift and forethought. Amounts from a penny upwards were received every Sunday afternoon in classroom 11. A bonus of sixpence in the pound was paid on each account, provided not more than three weeks in arrears. In that same year Seth Senior retired from being choir master, and marriages could take place at Milton Church without attendance of the registrar. The pastor in May 1899 was Revd J.S. Drummond of No. 8, Belgrave Terrace. Church Secretary Mr G.P. Stather of No. 26 Bath Street.

Below, left.
ON SUNDAY 22 November 1874, special services took place at St Patrick's Church to celebrate the redecoration. A beautiful stained glass memorial window in the Sanctuary was completed at a cost of £170. In 1891 Canon Dolan's Silver Jubilee in the priesthood took place, and a magnificent oak pulpit was unveiled in the church.

THE OLD VICARAGE, KIRKBURTON. Later converted into flats.

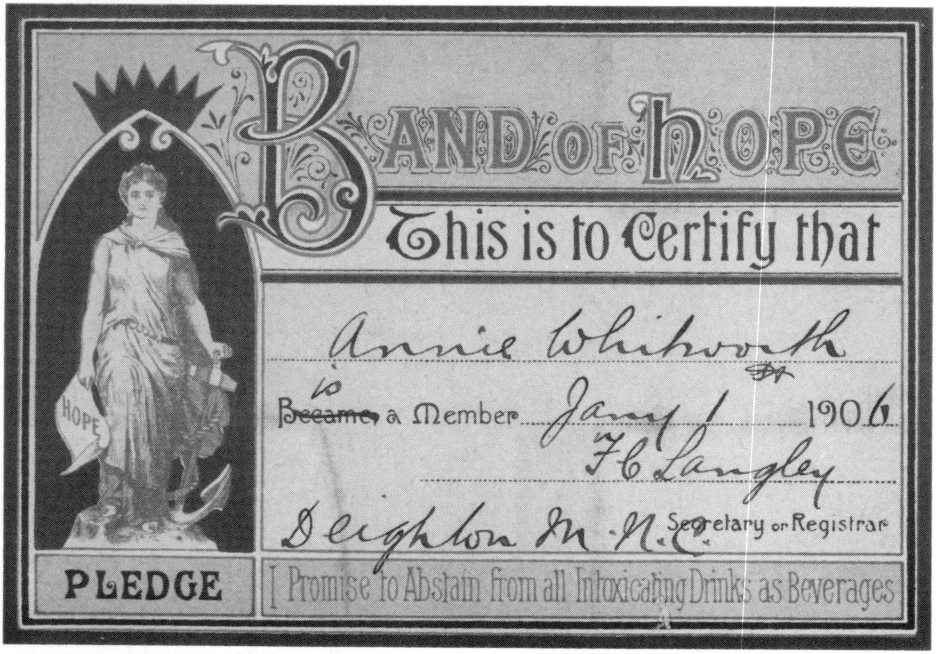

BAND OF HOPE

This is to Certify that

Annie Whitworth

~~Became~~ is a Member Jany 1 1906

F C Langley

Secretary or Registrar

Deighton M.N.C.

PLEDGE

I Promise to Abstain from all Intoxicating Drinks as Beverages

BAND OF HOPE PLEDGE. Nothing like a good resolution on New Year's Day! Annie kept her pledge until her dying day, apart from a small glass of ginger wine or sherry at Christmas time.

RASHCLIFFE CHURCH opened in 1864. Rashcliffe in those days was a 'stepped' terrace area, lit by gas. The writing over the archway interior reads, 'This is None Other but the house of God and this is the gate of heaven'.

BAPTIST CHAPEL, BIRKBY. The Baptist witness at Birkby began in a cottage before any of the other three free churches in the district. Two plots of land in Blacker Road were bought by auction for £141 on 13 August 1859 and conveyed by trust-deed to friends of Salendine Nook church on behalf of Birkby Baptist. On 5 June 1909, the foundation stone of the building in Wheathouse Road was laid.

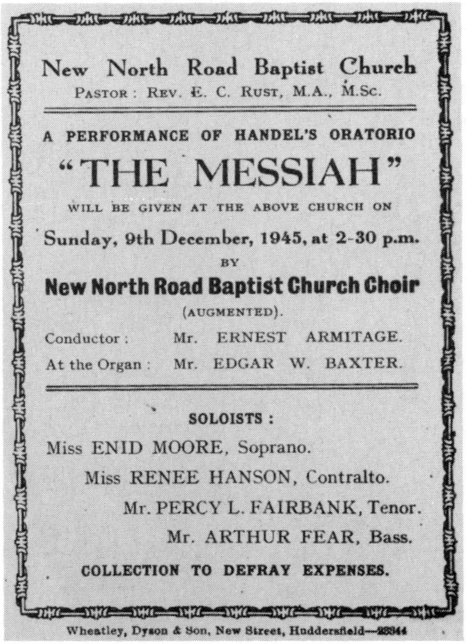

New North Road Baptist Church
PASTOR: REV. E. C. RUST, M.A., M.SC.

A PERFORMANCE OF HANDEL'S ORATORIO

"THE MESSIAH"

WILL BE GIVEN AT THE ABOVE CHURCH ON

Sunday, 9th December, 1945, at 2-30 p.m.

BY

New North Road Baptist Church Choir
(AUGMENTED).

Conductor: Mr. ERNEST ARMITAGE.
At the Organ: Mr. EDGAR W. BAXTER.

SOLOISTS:

Miss ENID MOORE, Soprano.
Miss RENEE HANSON, Contralto.
Mr. PERCY L. FAIRBANK, Tenor.
Mr. ARTHUR FEAR, Bass.

COLLECTION TO DEFRAY EXPENSES.

Wheatley, Dyson & Son, New Street, Huddersfield—26344

THE PROGRAMME COVER FOR 'THE MESSIAH' given in New North Road Baptist Church, Sunday 9 December 1945. Voices were raised in thanksgiving that the war was victoriously over in many such places of worship that year.

SHEEPRIDGE PROVIDENCE – great rival of Deighton Chapel.

PRIMROSE HILL CHURCH SCHOLARS, 16 May 1910. Only one person in the whole throng is without a hat, the lady in the passageway by the gas lamp.

MISS MARY PEARSON, Deighton Sunday School teacher and choir member. One look from her – or Blanche Chinn, who both sat in the same choir stalls every Sunday for years – and any talking or other misdemeanour, immediately stopped. Sucking 'Chapel Spice' (mint imperials) was one of the more usual crimes committed by Sunday school scholars, or the boys might decide to use a catapult, with Miss Pearson or Miss Chinn as the target. How daring they were! One memorable Sunday in class a group of boys even pulled the seat from under another teacher exactly at the moment she should have made contact with it. Who says Sunday schools are dull? Mrs Watson, though, laughed with them.

DEIGHTON UNITED METHODIST CHURCH. The original chapel was built around 1808, although the beginnings of Methodism in Deighton can be traced to a Wesleyan Society of 39 members recorded as being in existence in 1797. Deighton Chapel was the first to be erected for the Methodist New Connexion Denomination in all the wide area covered by the Huddersfield Circuit. Closing services in the old chapel were held on 2 January 1876. In 1913 the question of a new organ was discussed. Borough Organist Dr Arthur Pearson gave the first recital on the 'handsome new instrument' in the new chapel opened on 3 November 1915.

DEIGHTON SUNDAY SCHOOL ANNIVERSARY in June 1932, children's morning service held in the chapel. The theme that year, 'Count Your Blessings.' Oh the excitement of having a solo to sing! Front row: fifth left Barbara Norcliffe; Hazel Taylor, centre; Marie Clough, fifth right. Second row girls; second left, Barbara Wood, Dorothy Dyson (with head on one side). Opposite side, same row, blonde-haired Blanche Mellor. Row behind, Winifred Holmes, dark hair, next to Keith Priestley. Included in the choir stalls were Eric Hall, far right, and Kenneth Priestley next. Most children wore roses or carnations with fern cocooned in silver wrapping for the service, and the scent of flowers was delightful.

Below, left.

MEMBERS OF DEIGHTON CHAPEL in the early years of the century. John Taylor, grocer and draper, third left, seated. Trustees of the chapel since 1874 included George S. Poppleton, Joe Hampshire (he used to paint scenery for shows at Blackpool) William Cliff, Henry Langley, Allen Dyson, John P. Howarth, Donald Oddy, Wright Charlesworth, David Crawshaw, Harry Gibson and Ernest G. Taylor. In 1896 John Taylor was treasurer, his brother, Law Taylor, (mayor in 1924–6) was secretary in 1901. Arthur Nunn Priestley was organist from 1906.

QUEEN AND ATTENDANTS, DEIGHTON METHODIST SUNDAY SCHOOL, 1932 or 3. The cloaks were red velvet and then blue velvet on alternate years. Molly Dyson was the small attendant on the left; Jean Chadwick(?) seated next to Molly; Mary Poole, standing; Winifred Holmes (queen) another tall attendant flanking the queen, and Jean Poppleton seated next to the other small attendant, Hazel Taylor.

CHAPEL ON CHAPEL STREET, MOLDGREEN, demolished in 1989. Photograph taken in September 1913. On the back the message is 'Dear Cousin, your house is alright. A little box has come from Brighouse. A pipe is made up and we are almost flooded. It has poured down with rain all day. Hoping you are enjoying yourselves. Your cousin Annie.'

WEDDING OF FORMER HUDDERSFIELD FOOTBALLER, FRED LUNN, of the White Horse Inn, Leeds Road, to Ella Haigh, sister of Hilda, in 1932 or 1933. Winifred Halstead, in floral bridesmaid dress and picture hat is next to the bridegroom. Frank Brierley (?) is the pageboy and Hazel Taylor the small bridesmaid. I remember both of us pulling at the huge basketful of flowers, each trying to get the larger share. Weren't the gentlemen's winged collars smart?

THE WEDDING of Joe Taylor and the former Hilda Margaret Haigh at Deighton Chapel on 19 September 1923. Hilda's bouquet was of lilies. Her dress had been 'run up' by a local dressmaker. The wedding reception was held in the Sunday school. The Haigh family came to Huddersfield from Boroughbridge, and Joe first saw Hilda when she was in the choir at chapel. Right up to the date of her wedding, Hilda had to be home by ten o'clock in the evening. 'Anyone out after that time was up to no good', according to her mother.

WEDDING GROUP of Hilda and Joe Taylor at Deighton Chapel, 19 September 1923. Betsy Taylor is seated far left. Sarah Eleanor Haigh (bride's mother) third left. Bridesmaid Annie Whitworth is seated next to Joe. Ella Haigh is in the zig-zag patterned bridesmaid dress, fourteen-year-old Winifred Haigh is the other bridesmaid. Joe's mother Jane Taylor is seated next to Annie Brummit, far right. Standing, far right; Frank Walker, George Harold Brummit, John Taylor in tall silk hat, the bride's brother William next to her. Her father Arthur William Haigh is next to Revd Sheward. Huddersfield mayor-to-be Law Taylor (1924–6) far right on back row. Bride's brother George Haigh, in bowler hat, stands between the army man and John Taylor. The happy couple travelled by train from Huddersfield station to spend their honeymoon in a fisherman's cottage in Whitby.

SECTION EIGHT

Fashionable Huddersfield

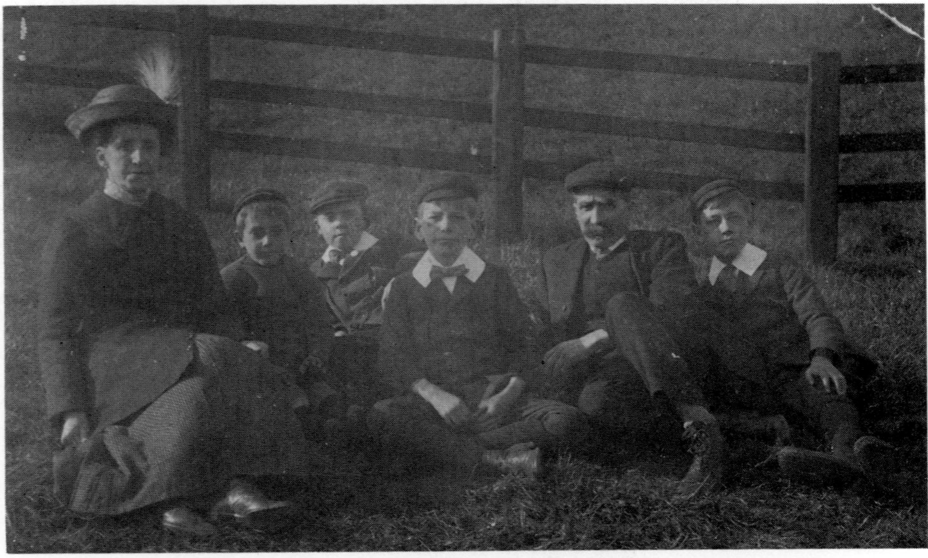

A DAY OUT IN THE LOCAL COUNTRYSIDE certainly did not call for slovenly or 'casual' dress prior to the First World War. This group included Frank Walker, next but one to the lady with the feather in her hat. Frank was affectionately known as 'Fatty Walker' to his chums. One of them being Joe Taylor, centre, and Alfred Taylor far right. In 1909 there were ten shirt makers in Huddersfield, including Leonard Osborne, Lion Arcade and John William Street and Charles Barrett, No. 4 Market Hall, King Street. There were dozens of tailors in town and surrounding district – Bairstow and Sons, Fitzwilliam Street; Booth and Sykes, Byrom Arcade, Station; Levi Gelder Street, 87 Church Lane, Moldgreen; Joe Cohen, No. 35 Ramsden Street and Grand Clothing Hall, Westgate and Railway Street. George Field, No. 11 John William Street, was a silk mercer.

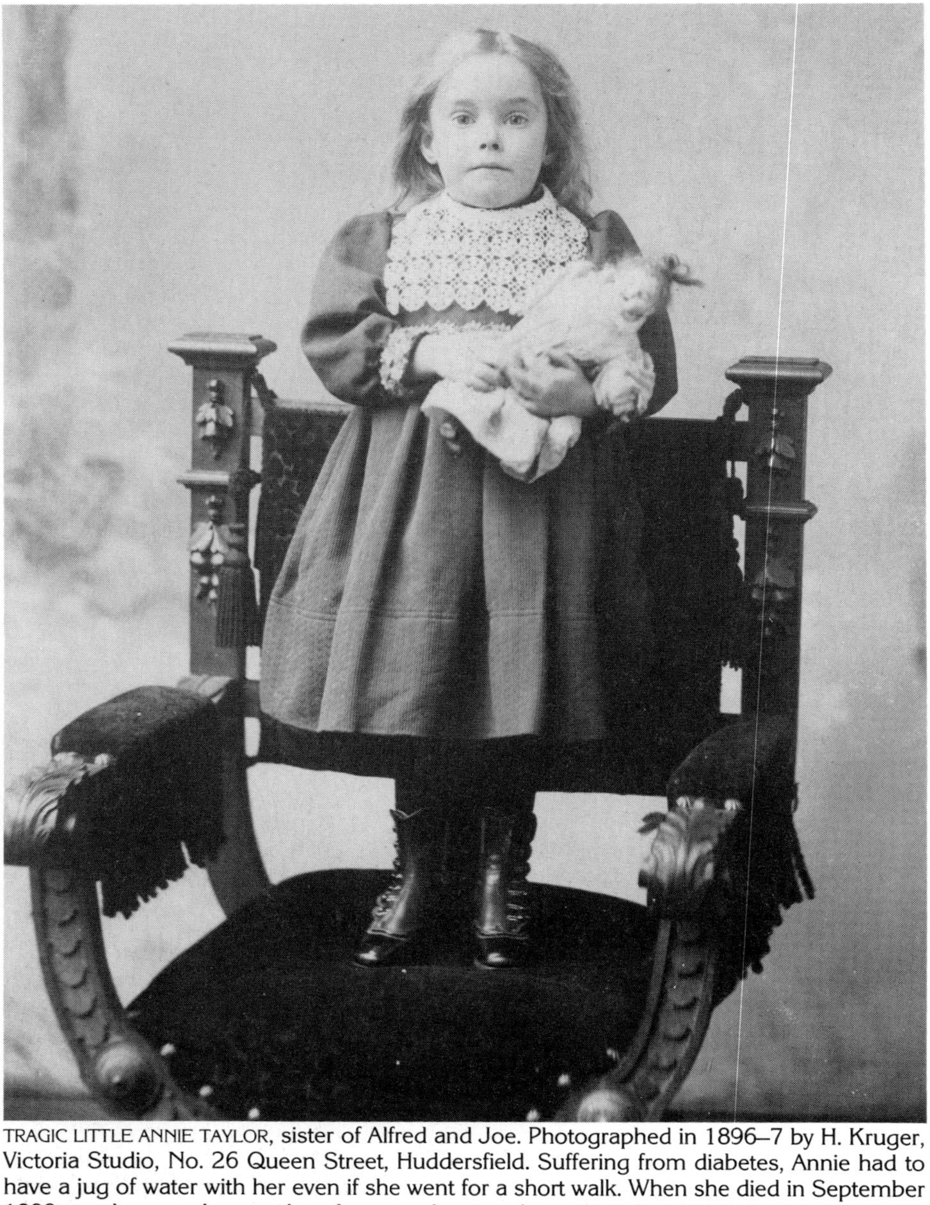

TRAGIC LITTLE ANNIE TAYLOR, sister of Alfred and Joe. Photographed in 1896–7 by H. Kruger, Victoria Studio, No. 26 Queen Street, Huddersfield. Suffering from diabetes, Annie had to have a jug of water with her even if she went for a short walk. When she died in September 1899 aged seven, her mother Jane put her two best china-headed dolls into two glass domes on the mantlepiece in the front room over the shop. Each Christmas new dresses were made for the dolls, then they were gently placed back in their glass domes for another year, in memory of Annie the little girl with the insatiable thirst. Even though the child could no longer be dressed in latest fashion, her dolls always were.

FRED WHITWORTH, who worked in a mill, Surr Samuel, and Hannah. Obviously posing in 'Sunday best' as clogs would be worn for work. Even 'working men' seemed to be able to afford a watch and chain, to wear proudly across the middle of a waist-coat. Perhaps they were handed down from father to son. Surely only a superb corset could manipulate that waist belonging to Hannah. In 1899 William Thomas, wholesale and retail draper, hosier etc. of No. 59 New Street, Huddersfield, advertised 'Every Requisite in Gents' Ties, Collars, Cuffs, shirts, pants etc. Reliable Makes in Kid and Fabric gloves, umbrellas, corsets, hosiery. Dressmaking, Mantle making, Millinery. A Trial solicited.' Poorer people pawned their best clothes at Claude Hill's, Chapel Hill.

THE WHITWORTH FAMILY, probably at home in Rastrick in the 1890s. Fred Whitworth seated, Hannah with baby Annie on her knee, Surr Samuel with protective hand on his mother's shoulder, George Harold Brummit and Elizabeth standing.

ANNIE WHITWORTH, photographed at H. Kruger's Victoria Studio, No. 26 Queen Street, Huddersfield. Annie remembered always having to wear a pinafore, after all, washing was hard work then. Clothes-horses, dripping with wet garments in bad weather were to be avoided as much as possible. And children – right up to the Second World War – usually had to change into 'second best' clothes after Sunday school.

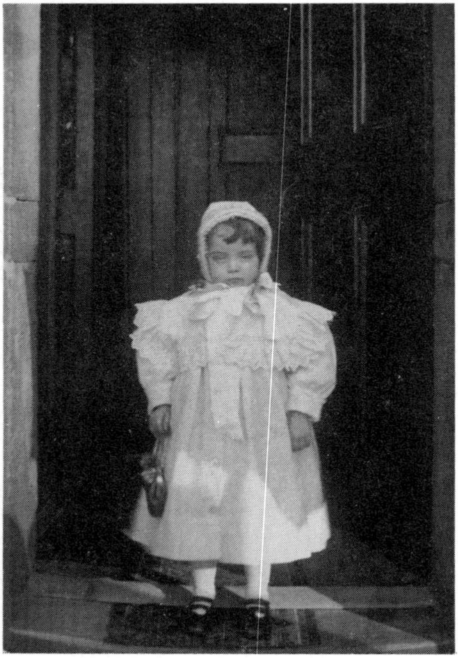

ANNIE WHITWORTH all dressed up in 1899. Her mother Hannah used to coax her daughter's hair into a fashionable 'kiss curl' over her forehead, and ringlets appeared after being curled with rags or tissue paper wound round the hair. Even doors looked different at that time, 'snecks' being the means of opening and shutting them – see the one behind Annie.

BEFORE SMALL, INEXPENSIVE CAMERAS became affordable to most, families saved up to try and have at least one childhood study taken in a 'proper' studio. Here is Surr Samuel Whitworth, photographed in around 1894 on a rocking horse belonging to the studio of W.C. Pearson, No. 24 Manchester Road, Huddersfield. Sam's brothers died in infancy within two days of each other during Whitsuntide 1891. Lest whopping-cough snatch Sam away without trace also, his mother made sure she had a photograph of him.

ANNIE WHITWORTH, left, and cousin Alice Taylor in 1898–9. It must have taken a long time doing up all the laces on Alice's boots. When Alice was seven she was so small she could walk upright beneath the kitchen table. Annie, a few years younger, appears to be the same height in the photograph.

LEG O'MUTTON SLEEVES emphasize the narrow waist of the dress worn by Elizabeth Brummit. When many families had no wealth to leave in wills, a favourite brooch was often bequeathed. When dresses were ankle-length a lady had no occasion to teeter about on high heeled shoes to be smart. In 1873 Mrs H. Liddell, Wholesale and Retail Boot and Shoe Manufacturer of No. 13 Market Place, advertised that 'Mrs. L. has always on hand, a Large Assortment of Ladies' and Gentlemen's Boots and Shoes of every description.' If ladies were troubled with bunions, they simply cut a piece out of the shoe or boot to allow the troublesome joint 'a bit of breathing space'. Many ladies were confined to their homes in wet weather because of the problem.

ELIZABETH BRUMMIT, studiously posed with a book (she may not even have been able to read it) – with nothing more exotic than a drainpipe as background. 'Modesty vests' were a popular item of clothing among the ladies. They could easily be removed for laundering, with far less toil than that required for the whole down-to-the-ankle dress.

JOHN AND JANE TAYLOR with Punch the dog in the back garden of Central Stores, Deighton. Sombre shades were the order of the day; striped trousers for John, black coat with stiff white collar, and inevitable watch-chain; Jane in long black dress. Make-up was definitely not worn by Jane ever.

ALFRED CASTLE TAYLOR, photographed by R.D. Shaw, of Deighton. He is holding a whip, the top to go with it out of view. In 1899 R. Worth & Co. of Nos. 29 & 31 King Street, had a large variety of new furs; rich sable necklets from 11*s.* 9*d.* to 9 guineas each, new styles in skunk, bear, marmot, mouflon, fox, opossum, and other skins from 11½*d.* to 4 guineas each. A large variety of the new storm collars for jackets from 1*s.*11½*d.* each were available plus a 'Special Show of Dress Goods in all the Latest Novelities.'

DEBONAIR YOUNG ALFRED TAYLOR. Enjoying the sartorial elegance that young men of the town were noted for. After all, the cloth from the area was unsurpassed. Add a straw boater, a slim walking cane, and you were fit to meet a king. At least, to fight for him.

JOE TAYLOR in around 1907. Charles Spencer, bootmaker, was in business at No. 68 Deighton Road at that time, and regularly 'heeled and soled' shoes and boots for local families. Joe would get his liberty bodices, night-shirts, socks and underwear from the big drapery drawers at his father's shop. Mending was a task that took up a great deal of time in those days, with socks being darned over wooden 'mushrooms'.

SAILOR SUITS, boaters, laced-up boots, 'Eton' collars and bow ties were the thing to wear for young boys in Edwardian Huddersfield. Joe and Alfred Taylor were photographed standing over a grate outside the living room-kitchen at the back of Central Stores.

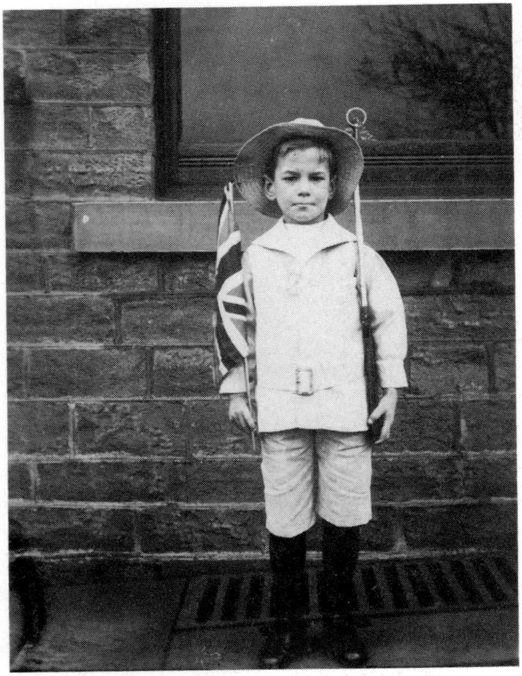

JOE TAYLOR IN SUMMER SAILOR SUIT, around 1908. The Union Jack he holds suggests it could have been Empire Day. In those stirring times school children proudly marched around school yards waving flags and singing patriotic songs. 'Land of Hope and Glory' and 'I Vow To Thee My Country', majestic tunes and words exactly right for inspiring that generation into joining up during the First World War which had burst upon that erstwhile peaceful Edwardian era.

BABY MARIE HAIGH with big sister, Eileen, pose for the photographer in 1926. The fashion then for small children was knitted garments and huge bows of ribbon to tie up the hair. The children's parents worked at a Slaithwaite mill, Mrs Haigh as a weaver, Mr Haigh a loom tuner. Marie was later to marry Roy Firth, one time conductor of Honley Male Voice Choir, and she enjoyed being a member of Huddersfield Vocal Union.

HILDA TAYLOR walking on New Street in the 1920s. One had to have hat pins in headgear then when riding on an open-topped tramcar or risk losing the hat.

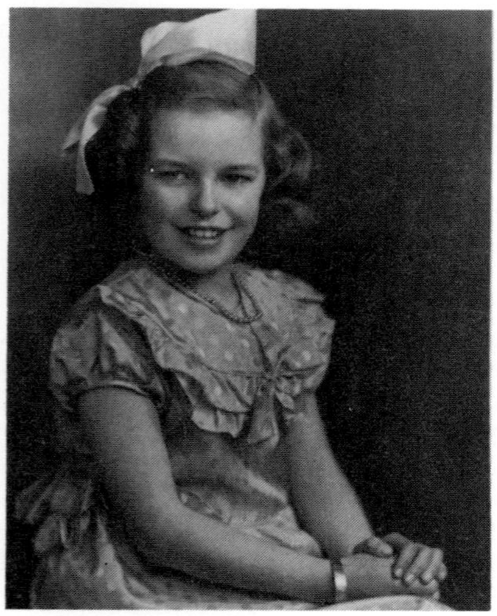

A PINK TAFFETA DRESS with huge matching bow for the hair worn by ten year old Hazel Taylor in 1937. A 'pearl' necklace and 'gold' bracelet added to the splendour of a new dress for Whitsuntide. Neighbours and relatives gave a penny to children when they called to show their new clothes. What heated arguments there were with mothers who insisted on liberty bodices being worn underneath if a 'nip' was in the air.

LISTEN WITH MOTHER. Elsie Wheeler of Linthwaite, with twins, Granville and Margaret in 1931–2. They had the thrill of a lifetime when, on *Children's Hour*, the announcer read their names over the air one birthday and said 'Happy Birthday, twins.' Mothers were rarely seen without some knitting 'on the go' in spare moments. Knitted suits and dresses for children were fashionable, with lots of 'pom-poms' for added interest.

AFTER THE SECOND WORLD WAR WAS OVER, the 'New Look' was eagerly adopted by Huddersfield girls. The new Mrs Philip Taylor, (née Audrey Cudworth), wore this turquoise gabardine outfit to travel by train on 5 July 1949 for her honeymoon. A flowered hat and platform shoes with ankle straps were 'up to the minute' fashion, as was the pouchy handbag.

SECTION NINE

Events

THE 'SOVEREIGN' BABIES GARDEN PARTY AT GATESGARTH, Lindley, 17 August 1907. Alderman and Mrs Broadbent gave a garden party for babies of Upperhead Row Section. In fine weather, a hundred good-looking, healthy babies, with mothers and some fathers, also guests, assembled in the grounds of the Deputy Mayor's house at Gatesgarth. Each baby was weighed, the heaviest being 29 lbs. (Weight was regarded as a good sign in those days.) Photographs were taken, and an excellent tea was enjoyed. Waggonettes were provided to and from the town. It was the second such party given by Mrs Broadbent. Benjamin Broadbent established the Infant Mortality Sub-Committee in Huddersfield. At the time of the garden party strawberry jam was 'ready at Wallaces branches, 1 lb. cost 5½*d*., 2 lbs. cost 10*d*.' Teacakes were still only eighteen for a shilling. Large arrivals of grouse were on sale at J.E. Wood, Son & Co. of Victoria Street. Fine value at 1*s*. 9*d*. each.

GREAT WOULD BE THE CONSTERNATION and the urge irresistible to 'go and have a look' when this tram accident happened at Bradley in the early years of the century. Those concerned could all have done with a cup of Wallaces' tea afterwards I bet!

DISASTER OFTEN STRIKES AT HOLIDAY TIME. This train collision occurred on Good Friday, 21 April 1905, between the Lancashire and Yorkshire passenger train driven by Wilfred Cliffe, or Mirfield, and the London and North Western Railway. Fred Haigh, of Hillhouse, was the driver of the latter. Two people were killed and several injured, Dr Crosland tended them.

Huddersfield Choral Society.

GRAND

Complimentary Concert

To Mr. Joshua Marshall (who is seriously ill)

Friday Evening, May 15th, 1885,

IN THE TOWN HALL.

Performance—MENDELSSOHN'S

"ELIJAH."

Principals :

Miss MARY DAVIES,

Miss WILKINSON, Miss HOLROYD,

Miss HILDA WILSON,

Miss ENGLAND, Mr. S. SCHOFIELD,

Mr. HENRY GUY,

Mr. F. HAIGH, Mr. B. STOCKS,

Mr. W. RILEY.

THE BAND AND CHORUS

WILL BE CONSIDERABLY AUGMENTED.

Leader .. .. Mr HENRY NUTTALL.
Grand Organ .. ..Mr. H. L. PARRATT.
Conductor .. .. Mr. JOHN NORTH.

Doors open at 6-45, Oratorio at 7-30 prompt. Tickets may be had and Plan of Hall may be seen at Messrs. Wood & Marshall's, New Street.

Balcony, 5/- Central Area (Reserved) 3/- Side Area, 2/.
Gallery and remainder of Hall, 1/-

J. EAGLETON, } Hon. Secs.
WM. DAWSON. }

OFFICERS are listed on the inside of this 1885 Choral Society concert programme. Part one had in it such wonderful music as a duet 'Zion spreadeth her hands' sung by Miss Mary Davies and Miss Hilda Wilson, Chorus – 'Lord, bow thine ear'.

ANNUAL GARDEN PARTY given by John and Jane Taylor in the market garden fields where they obtained fruit for making their renowned jams. John Taylor is fifth from the right with bald head and moustache. Jane is seated in front of him wearing a white blouse. Sitting by Jane's knees is Alice, the future Mrs Fred Bailey. Next but one along the row Alfred Taylor, boater hat in front of him, and brother Joe, also with hat on knee. Law Taylor far left, standing, with hand on hip.

A HAPPY BAND OF 'TRIPPERS' in the early 1930s. Popular singer of that time, Peter Dawson, is advertised on a placard on the photograph. Jane Taylor, wrapped in huge fur (she was then plagued with rheumatism) with Annie Brummitt, also in a fur wrap. Keeping draughts at bay, in the years before central heating, was almost a full time occupation with some elderly ladies.

GENERAL FRENCH on the way to unveil the Fallen Heroes Memorial in Greenhead Park, on 20 May 1905, driving through Westgate. The Boer War claimed the lives of 28 men from Huddersfield and district. On the day of the unveiling, a keen wind blew up from the east. The mayor had asked trades people to decorate their premises with flags and bunting.

HAVING A PHOTOGRAPH TAKEN was an event to dress up for in the latter years of the nineteenth century. It is now almost a century since this photograph of John and Jane Taylor, with baby Annie, was posed for, the original is quite scratched. The bucket and spade, held by Jane, suggests that they were either going to the seaside or already there. John wears formal striped trousers and watch-chain across his waistcoat; little Annie, who died in infancy was so muffled up she can scarcely be seen at all.

SPECIAL ATTRACTIONS
at the Exhibition you must not miss

In the DRILL HALL

Daily, at 3-0 and 7-0 p.m.:

"BEAUTY AND FASHION OF 1935," presented by "EUGENE," featuring IVY TRESMAND, the Famous Musical Comedy Star; IRENE ASHTON (Miss 1900) and MARY JUNE (Miss 1935), in their Novel Act, "COMPARISONS."

February 16th and 23rd, at 2-15 and 6-15:

Displays of TAP DANCING, GREEK DANCING, etc., by members of the Women's League of Health and Beauty, Huddersfield Branch.

In the TEMPERANCE HALL

CONTINUOUS

Health Cookery Demonstrations

DAILY

By Messrs. PENTSALES, LTD., 6, Jewry Street, London.

THE TEMPERANCE HALL AND DRILL HALL held many exhibitions. Mabel Glover had a dancing academy at No. 70 New North Road. Cambridge Road Baths were opened in 1931, and dances were held there in wintertime.

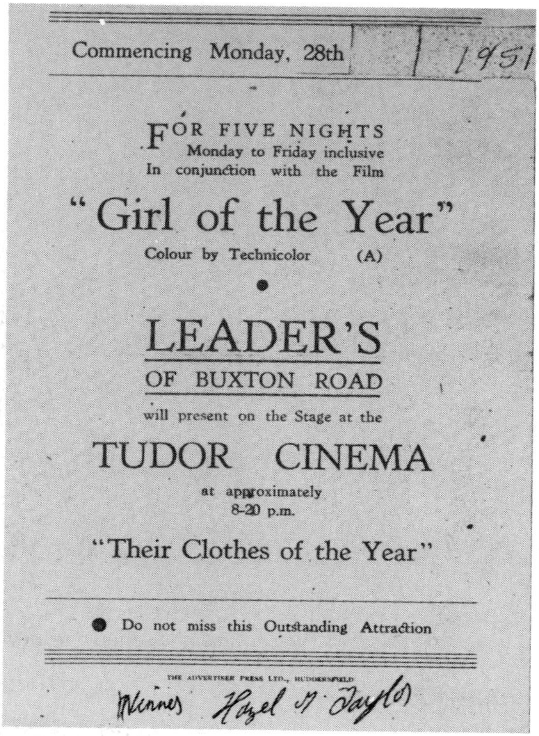

Commencing Monday, 28th | | 1951

FOR FIVE NIGHTS
Monday to Friday inclusive
In conjunction with the Film

"Girl of the Year"

Colour by Technicolor (A)

●

LEADER'S
OF BUXTON ROAD

will present on the Stage at the

TUDOR CINEMA

at approximately
8-20 p.m.

"Their Clothes of the Year"

● Do not miss this Outstanding Attraction

THE ADVERTISER PRESS LTD., HUDDERSFIELD

Winner Hazel M. Taylor

THE TUDOR CINEMA, Ramsden Street, attracted audiences on Friday, 1 June 1951 by holding a competition, 'Girl of the Year'. Lady Martin presented a voucher for £7 to spend on a dress from Leaders of Buxton Road, also a crate of fruit juices, to Hazel Taylor, the winner. Mr Clark was Manager of the Tudor.

ROYALTY HAVE OFTEN VISITED THE TOWN. Here is Princess Margaret, with Town Hall officials, in 1970 outside the orchestra entrance to the Town Hall. Joan Donnolly and her guide-dog presented a bouquet to the princess inside. Princess Margaret officially opened the new market hall and the welfare centre.

THE OLD POLICE STATION AND CROWN COURT (facing) on Peel Street. Modern buildings have since replaced the police station building. Probably one of the most unpleasant events in anyone's life is to be summoned to appear in court. In 1988 Hazel Wheeler became the first juror to object to other jurors smoking while waiting to go into court. Because 'smoking could distract her, and not smoking while waiting for a case to begin could disturb smokers,' she was excused from any further service by Judge Robert Taylor.

THE FALLEN HEROES MEMORIAL in Greenhead Park, which was unveiled by General French in 1905. It is garlanded with wreaths and poppies on Armistice Day.

ON SATURDAY, 15 September 1951, members of the Taylor family had a reunion in Deighton Sunday School to welcome Eva and her American husband. Eva, niece of Law Taylor, went to America some years previously to visit Aunt Carrie, sister of Law and John. On the boat she met her future husband, William Wilson, and Florida became her home. Among the guests were Annie Whitworth, seated, far right, Hazel Taylor next to her. Mrs Alice Bailey is next to Eva, centre, with her husband William. Wilf Cliffe is third row back fifth left – he was the driver of the train that collided on Good Friday 1905. Jack Boothroyd, third row, standing, between Eva and Alice who are seated on the row in front. Ernest Taylor (son of Law Taylor) second right on the back row, and Harry Gibson fourth right, back row. Molly, Law Taylor's daughter, wears a check dress on the front row.

Below, left.
CHRISTMAS, 1937, and a family get together in the back room behind Central Stores, Deighton. Hilda Taylor wearing paper cap from a cracker, daughter Hazel on her knee. (Blowing one of those infernal toy trumpets!) Winifred Halstead tells son Brian to 'look at the camera' and the shop's live-in maid Alice Roebuck gets ready to help wash up. Marion Haigh (Hilda's sister-in-law) also has her 'pinny' on ready to help, while Kenneth Halstead, (for a change!) is on the other side of the camera.

ONE OF THE MOST POPULAR EVENTS was the Children's Talent Show. Heats were held every Thursday evening from mid-July to the final in late August. Six-year-old Elizabeth, and four-year-old Caroline Wheeler, were in the final on 20 August 1960. For their interpretation of 'Get me to the Church on Time' they received a silver cup and 32*s*. The official programme for Huddersfield Summer Entertainments cost 3*d*. that year.

SECTION TEN

Entertaining Huddersfield

IN THE HEYDAY OF OPERETTAS, the 1920s and '30s, many were produced in Deighton Sunday School. Including *Highwayman Love* (oh, that lovely lilting song 'Phillida' included!), *HMS Pinafore, Her Ladyship, Rajah of Rajapoure* and others. What shivers of excitement ran through the audience if they had anyone related to them in the operetta, as snatches of music were played before the curtain went slowly up – then, what torrents of applause and demands for 'encore!' as the curtain came down. Flowers galore were sent up on stage in tribute, to be graciously accepted by the principals, who were really into the swing of it all on the final evening, and sorry to have to return to being ordinary mortals come the following week. The majority of the audience were locals or staying with friends or relatives, so few problems arose regarding transport home. They walked home afterwards, happily humming songs from the show. Henry Dryer is far left, Stanley Dawson, Dorothy Priestley, Winifred Holmes, Joe Taylor, and Mary Dyson, in 1932.

OPERETTA AT DEIGHTON. Line up for photographs on the final evening. David Crawshaw, kneeling, far left, next to Joyce Walker Sunday school teacher Blanche Chinn kneeling between the 'Indian' girls; Marjorie Wood, Jean Woodworth, Jean Chadwick. Standing, far right, Allan Dyson, Olive Crawshaw, Frank Woodworth, Dorothy Priestley, Donald Oddy, Louie Haggis, Stanley Dawson, Norrie Woodworth, Vera Whitehead, Joe Taylor (wearing wig) Mary Pearson, Harold Charlesworth, Arthur Nunns Priestley (choir master). Also on the photograph are Dorothy Walker, Madge Brook, Vera Knapton, Harry Hall, Hilda Gibson, Tom Jessop, Henry Dryer, Wright Charlesworth and Basil Croft.

MADAM CLARA BUTT'S CONCERT TO CHILDREN OF HUDDERSFIELD in the Town Hall, 6 March 1907. It was part of the Subscription Concerts, single admission, reserved seats cost 5*s.* and 2*s.* 6*d.*, unreserved orchestra 2*s.*, gallery 1*s.* It was part of Clara and her husband, Kennerley Rumford's, provincial tour prior to their world tour. Paderewski gave a Grand Pianoforte Recital in the Town Hall on 15 October that year.

Opposite.
LANCE KEY, THEN PRESIDENT OF THE MUSICIAN'S UNION, of No. 109 Bradford Road, explaining how to play the Serpent to youngest daughter Wendy in 1938. During the Second World War Lance Key was Area Organizer of the Musician's Union. Prior to the fire at the Palace Theatre in 1936, he played the cello there. Lance was a founder member of the Galpin Society, and a keen collector of old musical instruments. His eldest daughter, Betty, played the trombone in Lindley Boys' Band in the forties – they were so glad to have an excellent trombone player that the fact she wasn't the right sex had to be overlooked. Betty could also have joined Ivy Benson's All Girls Band – but Dad thought that Betty playing away from home, might have been a little too risky!

LONGWOOD CO-OP JUBILEE CARNIVAL, 1909.

WAS THIS A MAY DAY CELEBRATION? Cissie Ferguson (second right, back row) later became a Huddersfield school teacher, and married Brooke Dews, of Crosland Moor.

SIR MALCOLM SERGENT, conductor of Huddersfield Choral for many years. He quoted in the programme to honour his 70th birthday, 29 April 1965, 'Music is yesterday, today, and tomorrow. Each age is a dream that is dying, or one that is coming to birth.' And from Elgar's Music Makers:–

Great hail! we cry to the comers,
From the dazzling unknown shore
Bring us hither your sun and summers
And renew our world, as of yore
You shall teach us your songs new numbers
And things that we dreamed not before;
Yea, in spite of a dreamer who slumbers,
And a singer who sings no more."

ELLA HAIGH, who won the Mrs Sunderland Rose Bowl at Huddersfield Town Hall in the 1920s. The Mrs Sunderland competition began as a tribute to a Brighouse singer, born in 1819, Susan Sykes. She married Henry Sunderland and had six children. When invited by Queen Victoria to sing at Buckingham Palace, her Majesty remarked 'I am the Queen of England, but you are the Queen of Song.' The first Mrs Sunderland Musical Competition was held in Huddersfield Town Hall in 1889.

COLNE VALLEY MALE VOICE CHOIR. In a rural setting following the first of their wins in 1960 at the International Eisteddfod in Llangollen, 1960. George Stead holds the trophy. Roy Firth is to the right of the photograph, standing. George Stead is one of England's finest choral trainers. He often said that, 'music is a gift from God, and anyone possessing that gift should endeavour to perfect it, to make it more acceptable to him who gave the gift.'

Below, right.
COLNE VALLEY MALE VOICE CHOIR in 1963 when they were visited by the Rhos Male Voice Choir. Photographed outside Golcar Baptist Church. Roy Firth, one time conductor of the Honley Male Voice Choir, is second left, front row. Conductor George Stead standing, second left behind front row. The choir frequently sings in the Town Hall.

HOLME VALLEY MALE VOICE CHOIR was formed in 1910 by Irving Silverwood. He is seated on the front row, holding the baton.

HUDDERSFIELD CO-OP CHOIR. Ronnie Daniels, conductor, far left, front row; Joan Donaldson, second left, standing; Hilda Hulme, far right, next to back row; Hilda Gregory, centre, next to back row; Sydney Gregory, second right, back row. Joan Donaldson is a well-known figure in Huddersfield, with her guide dog.

MEMBERS OF HUDDERSFIELD VOCAL UNION. Marie Firth, fifth left, seated on the front row. George Stead, conductor, centre, front row. The Union began as the Geldholt Vocal Union in 1913. Their first success, under the direction of Mr J. Fletcher Sykes, was in 1914 when they came second to the Colne Valley Vocal Union at New Brighton. They secured first prizes at the Welsh Eisteddfod in 1917 and 1925, and have gained prizes at Blackpool, Wharfedale, Morecambe, Halifax and Mrs Sunderland competitions.

Below, left.
MARSDEN BOYS' BAND. Ready to tour South Africa in the British Empire Boys' Band. Left to right: Bobby Brown (drum major), Ronald Ball (cornet), Jack Worsnip (soprano), Ronald Matley (baritone). (Should the soprano really be tenor?)

THE LATE JOE WOOD, long time secretary of Huddersfield Authors' Circle, with his wife Alice, Kathleen Binns, speaker at the literary luncheon, and the late Marjorie Wilkinson, of Follett Avenue, Beaumont Park. Marjorie was a well-known speaker on local history. Joe enjoyed writing detective stories.

FORMER MEMBERS OF HUDDERSFIELD AUTHORS' CIRCLE. Dr S.L. Henderson-Smith, leaning forward; right, Dorothy Crawshaw at the head of table; Susan Richardson in flowered hat; Bob Richardson and Mrs Shaw – grandmother of Huddersfield's academic prodigy, Ruth Lawrence. The group was at a literary luncheon in Wrigleys Café. Dr S.L. Henderson-Smith writes poetry and frequently contributes to the *Huddersfield Examiner* letters' column and other newspapers.

HUDDERSFIELD YOUTH ORCHESTRA trip to Ilkley in the 1960s, led by Harold Newcombe, former Head of Instrumental Music and conductor of the Senior Youth Orchestra.

ELIZABETH WHEELER, one time member of Huddersfield Youth Orchestra, practising the violin in the garden of her home, Greenhead Lane, Dalton.

DEIGHTON SECONDARY SCHOOL in March 1967, gave an outstandingly successful performance of Gilbert and Sullivan's *Patience*. The orchestra was that of Huddersfield College of Technology directed by Mr C.F. Sutcliffe, the show was produced by Mr D. Smithson. Mr F. Burns was headmaster. Patience was played by Ann Fairclough, standing, far left. Ladies of the chorus included: Elizabeth Wheeler, Julie Moon, Audrey Mansfield, Susan North, Christine Devlin and Norma Fletcher. Mr Shaw taught the violin at Deighton School of Music. That success was followed in March 1970 with a magnificent *Mikado* by the pupils. Again, music was provided by members of the College of Technology School of Music and the Senior Youth Orchestra. John Ellis played Ko-Ko, the Lord High Executioner; Howard Habron, Pooh-Bah; Graham Ellin was the Mikado; Julie Moon 'Katisha' and Elizabeth Wheeler and Audrey Mansfield were Pitti-Sing and Peep-Bo.

THELMA PIGGOTT (LATER BARLOW) AND JOE BERRY in Huddersfield Thespians' *The Glass Menagerie* in 1950. The Thespians began in the Manager's office of the Theatre Royal in 1920, when James R. Gregson was manager of the theatre. Andrea Woolner, a teacher at Greenhead High School, was one of the first leading lights – Edith Spikes, music mistress, also joined, and Miss New and Miss Gilmore were committee members. Miss Beatrice Beard, also at Greenhead, was in the 1920 cast of *Quality Street* performed at the Theatre Royal before Christmas that year.

THELMA PIGGOTT in *The Glass Menagerie*, 1950. Thelma was brought up in Huddersfield from the age of six. She attended first Birkby Council then Longley Hall School for Girls, living in Moldgreen then Aldmondbury. Thelma decided to take the drama and speech training course at 'tech' after leaving school. Before turning professional, Thelma worked as a secretary, lastly with Eddison, Taylor and Booth. Joe Berry was her first drama lecturer. Mrs Mary Whitfield taught speech training and Thelma was first in the 'Mrs Sunderland' elocution class in the Town Hall in 1949.

HOPE BANK, HONLEY, UNITED SING, 2 August 1908. J.W. Mellor, President of the Sing committee, said that the 'infant had grown seven years.' Among the well-loved tunes were the Twelfth Mass by Mozart and 'Stand up, Stand up for Jesus'.

DOES THE FACE OF THE ADULT BRIDESMAID LOOKS FAMILIAR? It is 'Mavis' of TV's *Coronation Street*, Thelma Barlow, at the wedding of her sister Veda to Mr Alastair McGhee, in the early fifties. Best man was Gerald Hirst. Small bridesmaid, Lindsay Laverick, is cousin of Thelma and Veda.

HAZEL TAYLOR PARTNERED BY ANDREW KIE-DROWSKI (right) at a formal dance in Huddersfield Town Hall – long gloves and evening dress was worn by some! In the late forties people were wanting to forget clothes rationing and austerity. Arnold Hoyle, left, emigrated to New Zealand.

WHEN THIS PHOTOGRAPH WAS TAKEN, at a Cambridge Road Baths dance in 1948, the 'Big Bands' were all the rage, as were jive and jitterbug dancing. Pictured are Eileen Robinson, left, Joyce Wise, Ivan Eastwood, Hazel Taylor and friends. The Squadronnaires Broadcasting Band drew large crowds to the Baths on Monday 15 January 1945, when not so much dancing was done as standing round the dais listening in admiration.

THE PICTURE HOUSE, RAMSDEN STREET. In 1937 the manager was Mr F. Carter. Cinemas abounded when, in 1935, the building of the 'Ritz' began. It was here that Jimmy Ainley proudly emerged, seemingly from the bowels of the earth, bowing to each side of the audience as he played the organ before the film started, at the town's latest and 'poshest' cinema, with restaurant attached. The Empire, Princess, Tudor, and Grand, were among those in the town centre. The Waterloo, Regent, Rialto, Regal and Lyceum numbered among those in Huddersfield districts. In 1916 it cost 2*d*., 3*d*., 4*d*., 6*d*. or 9*d*. to go to the Lockwood Picture Palace.

PALACE THEATRE, KIRKGATE, first opened in 1909. Atkin Baker was musical director in the 1940s. He was always immaculate in evening suit and bow tie. Pupils of Miss Richardson's Dancing School were included in a programme for April 1927. Gloria Gaye and her Glamour Girls Band 'Bringing you Sweet Music and Hot Rhythm' appeared in 1940. Henry Hall and his band played at the Palace in 1945. Free passes were issued to shopkeepers for two people each week, in return for displaying the Palace programme in a prominent position. The old building was burnt down in 1936. It is now a bingo hall.

SECTION ELEVEN

Politics and People

HAROLD WILSON, the boy who lived at Cowlersley, attended Royds Hall School, and later became Prime Minister. On this 1970 photograph he is with the Head Girl of Colne Valley High School, Linda Firth, and the then Head Boy, Andrew Harrison. When Harold Wilson was fourteen he spent a camping holiday at Honley. With some other lads he went to a local farm for some milk. Twelve of the boys, including the future Prime Minister, became infected with typhoid, and were taken to Meltham Isolation Hospital as it then was. Six of the youngsters died. Harold's grandfather was said to have remarked 'that lad's been spared for something'.

JOHN TAYLOR, grocer and draper, brother of Law. John, a Liberal, was violently opposed to the political standpoint of Law Taylor, and stood for the Municipal election in 1920. A lifelong teetotaller, he served as a trustee for Deighton Methodist Chapel. If a customer was 'hard up' was always ready to give a bag of broken biscuits or 'tick' until times were better.

LAW TAYLOR WAS THE FIRST LABOUR MAYOR OF HUDDERSFIELD, 1924–6. Son of Deighton market gardener Abel Taylor, Law's early education was at Deighton Board School. He left when 13 to work as a woollen piecener. In 1889 he became a postman, in 1915 he was appointed assistant inspector of postmen. For twenty years he was secretary of Huddersfield Postmen's Federation, ultimately becoming general treasurer for the whole country. In 1906 he was elected labour representative of the Dalton, Deighton, and Bradley ward by nine votes. He was elected to the aldermanic bench in 1920. Among varied public services, Law Taylor was always devoted to the humanistic side of the Council's activities.

ANNIE WHITWORTH, seated, and her cousin Cissie Ferguson when they were pupils at Greenhead Municipal High School for Girls. Annie and her widowed mother went to live with her cousins Joe and Alfred at Central Stores, Deighton, for a while. Mrs Whitworth, (who had been taking in washing to keep her home going and Annie at High School), helped in the shop and house. Hannah Whitworth was proud that she had been able, through her own endeavours, to allow her daughter to attend college and later enter the teaching profession.

GEORGE HERBERT HIRST, S. HAIGH AND WILF RHODES. Wilf Rhodes and George Herbert Hirst were famous cricketers at a time when local youth 'ate, drank, and dreamed cricket'. When the two were asked who they thought was the greatest cricketer, Hirst replied that it was Rhodes, Rhodes declined to say.

BLAKE LEE GUEST HOUSE, Marsden, was a favourite meeting place in the early years of the century. On 2 October 1905, Joseph Woodhead, Wilf Rhodes (born 1877), G. Hirst (born in Kirkburton 1871) and S. Haigh enjoyed a rendezvous at Blake Lee. Joseph, son of Godfrey Woodhead, currier and leather merchant, was born at Pog Inn, Holmfirth on 8 May 1824. He lectured on temperance platforms, and became absorbed in the controversy raging about the Great Reform Bill. In around 1850 the idea of a newspaper advocating the new Liberalism was born. Joseph Woodhead was invited to edit the paper, the *Huddersfield Examiner* which still flourishes. He was mayor of the town in 1883, and President of the Glee and Madrigal Society for some years.

EDITH ANN KEY of No. 109 Bradford Road, was branch secretary and organizer of the Huddersfield branch of the Womans' Social and Political Union. An important figure in the fight for votes for women, Edith was well-known to Mrs Pankhurst, who used to visit her home. The wife of Charles Key, a 6ft tall, blind piano tuner, her granddaughters Betty and Wendy were told never to miss using their vote, as their grandmother had helped fight for it. The big event in 1908 was a demonstration in St George's Square on Sunday 27 September. No less than 20,000 people attended. Mr and Mrs Key had a music shop in West Parade, as well as Bradford Road. Suffragettes held their inaugural meeting on January 1907 at Robinson's café. There was a later meeting at The Friendly and Trades Club, then the Clarion café. Edith Key died in 1938.

ANOTHER HUDDERSFIELD CAMPAIGNER, this time against fluoride being added to the water supply. Mrs Joyce Woodhouse, of Brian Avenue, Dalton, is also a regular contributor to the *Huddersfield Examiner* letters page, and a member of the town's Authors' Circle. Joyce was photographed outside Oaklands, formerly an Old People's Home, Greenhead Lane, Dalton.

A PORTRAIT OF HILDA TAYLOR, by Greaves Studio of No. 55, New Street, in the thirties. The Halifax photographer began the studio in Huddersfield in April 1919, with Willie Naylor in charge. In its early years one could have a choice of two proofs and twelve postcards sepia toned for 7*s*. 6d., or six for 4*s*. 6*d*. It used to be quite an occasion to have one's portrait taken. The present Mr Naylor, Philip, recalls a woman in the late twenties ushering in a little lad. 'I want him chopping off by t'stocking tops' she commanded.

FILM STAR JAMES MASON was born at Marsh, Huddersfield. After Cambridge University he entered the acting profession. He arrived in Hollywood in 1947, aged 38. 'There was something electric, and at the same time very dangerous about James', actress Ann Todd said. (Could be applied to a few more Huddersfield born and bred people too!) His more famous films included *The Seventh Veil, The Man in Grey* and *The Wicked Lady*; he died in 1984, aged 75.

PHILIP TAYLOR, clerk at the National Provincial Bank in King Street during the war years. In the photograph he is wearing his ARP badge. Falling off a bicycle with faulty brakes when fourteen almost cost Philip his life and precluded his ambition of joining the RAF. An 'Old Boy' of Huddersfield Boys' College, Philip later worked in banks in Sheffield, Sutton Coldfield, Shipley, Mansfield, and finally was bank manager of the National Westminster branch in Great Yarmouth. He died aged 52 on 16 May 1978.

CISSIE FERGUSON, LATER MRS BROOKE DEWS, of Crosland Moor – the couple lived on Blackmoorfoot Road. This photograph was taken by Greaves, of No. 55 New Street and judging by the style of dress it was most likely taken in the early twenties. Cissie was a teacher in Huddersfield schools before retiring, and a keen chapel-goer. Regularly Cissie and Brooke went to Guernsey, in the Channel Islands, for holidays, but were always happy to return to home – and to Park Road Methodist.

GEOFFREY'S PHOTOGRAPHIC STUDIO on New Street was a quick, informal place to pop into during the 1940s. It was especially useful for servicemen and women who had no time when on leave to book appointments. I think people could have three photographs for half a crown there in those days. Hilda Taylor, fond of following fashion, was willing to forego the formal 'Kay Francis' look for a Deanna Durbin hairstyle with ribbons, and typical padded-shoulder dress of the era for this Geoffrey's snapshot. She needed plenty of snaps to send abroad to soldiers and others who visited the grocer's shop directed there from the Huddersfield YMCA when seeking civilian hospitality.

GENIAL JOE TAYLOR, proprietor of Central Stores until his death in September 1948. Joe a one-time pupil at Huddersfield College, passed the entrance exam to Cambridge University and was all set to become a chemist, then the First World War changed everyone's plans. Alfred, his older brother, died of 'spotted fever' and meningitis in army camp at Rugeley, and Joe had to help his ageing parents at the shop. However, he proved a blessing to some of the customers, not well up in the 'three R's'. Often, if an important letter needed to be written, they asked him to do it. One was threatened with a solicitor's letter, and was quite perturbed. Would Joe help her? 'Who are your solicitors – Freeman, Hardy, and Willis?' he wrote. The customer never heard another thing about the affair. This photograph is an enlarged 'Polyfoto', 48 on a sheet. During the war there was a Polyfoto studio on New Street.

SECTION TWELVE

Parks and Beauty Spots

THE MUSEUM, RAVENSKNOWLE PARK. The first recorded mention of 'Ravensknolle' on Wakefield Road does not occur until 1444. The name probably derives from an Anglo-Saxon or Viking settler named 'Hrafu' – the raven. By the nineteenth century Ravensknowle was a small farmhouse on the Dalton estate. John Beaumont, manufacturer of fancy waistcoating, bought the estate between 1859 and 1862. He built a house, Ravensknowle Hall, 'at a cost of more than £20,000'. In 1901 it was purchased by Leigh Tolson. Later he gave the hall to the people of Huddersfield as a museum and memorial to his two nephews who were killed in the First World War. Robert Huntriss Tolson was killed on the first day of the Battle of the Somme in 1916 and James Martin at Solesme only three weeks before the Armistice in 1918. The museum was opened in 1922.

MOORLANDS REFRESHMENT ROOMS, 'Good Stabling.' Above Outlane, this establishment still caters for hungry and thirsty travellers. Oh, to see ladies and gentlemen dressed with such elegance again! Parasols, panama hats, walking canes – and good manners.

AN OUTING TO NONT SARAH'S has long been popular. The name is a colloquialism for aunt. In the middle of the last century a native of Scammonden (the hostelry is near the dam) took over the moorland inn. Then named the Coach and Horses, it was in a dilapidated condition, but the landlord was short of money. Then his beloved Aunt Sarah came to his assistance – and the landlord ever after extolled the virtues of his 'Nont Sarah'. In around 1870 a Mrs Sykes took over the tenancy, and had the name Coach and Horses officially changed to honour 'Nont Sarah'. Sarah's ghost is reputed to have been encountered more than once in the cellar.

GREENHEAD PARK was opened in 1884. Amenities included a bandstand, where extracts from Gilbert and Sullivan and other stirring tunes of the day entertained smartly dressed 'promenaders'. Children could sail boats on the lake, and immaculately laid out flower beds delighted the eye. No one would have ever dreamed of vandalizing flowers or other public property in those days, or throwing litter. Tennis courts, a children's playground, (a memorial to Richard Oastler, the 'Factory King'), Italian gardens and bowling greens are other attractions of Greenhead Park.

BEAUMONT PARK was opened by the Duke and Duchess of Albany in 1883. The first sod was cut in 1880, at the time the Poor Law offices were opened (they were in Ramsden Street). Beaumont Park is regarded by many as Huddersfield's most natural park. It lies in the wooded valley that runs up to Meltham. The site was presented by Mr H.F. Beaumont.

GRIMSCAR WOOD, near Birkby. Another popular venue for those seeking peace and solitude, and perhaps an armful of bluebells in May-time.

PACKING A WICKER PICNIC BASKET and heading for the open spaces of Blake Lee, Marsden, a delightful beauty spot to visit in limited leisure time. Walking was then, and still is, one of the cheapest and finest means of combating what is now referred to as stress. Better by far than drugs.

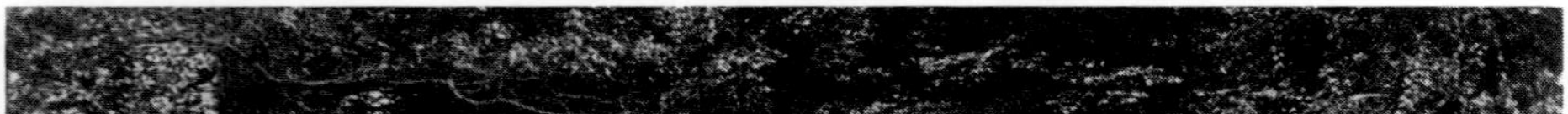

AS AN ALTERNATIVE TO MOORLAND PANARAMAS, tramping through Mollicar Woods, Farnley Tyas, was enjoyable. Ancient wooden stiles, rippling streams, and occasional glimpses of sky through the thickly wooded area lent enchantment to the scene.

GREENHEAD PARK, near Trinity Church and within easy walking distance of the town centre, has been the venue for varied entertainments and contests: donkey rides, roundabouts, bowling matches, flower and vegetable shows and during wartime 'Holidays at Home'. Simply a pleasant place to go if one couldn't afford to go away on holiday.

WESSENDEN VALLEY. A tramcar ride up to Marsden, then the joy of taking great gulps of fresh air walking over Wessenden, another favourite place to visit. Half day closing used to be on Wednesday in Huddersfield. 'Going up Wessenden' must have been something to look forward to all week, especially for those working in the stifling heat of the mills and factories. However, it would have been out of the question on the Sabbath – that was for chapel or church.

A MULTI-VIEW OF HUDDERSFIELD, in an evergreen surrounded frame, 1905. On the first, horses and carts are drawn up outside the station. The second top scene is of the lake in Beaumont Park. The left-hand photograph shows an open-topped tramcar in St George's Square, centre, the Market Square with horse and cart, ladies in ankle-length dresses and gentlemen in bowler hats and others in cloth caps. Rushworth's corner, Westgate is next at its splendid best. Despite the evergreen decoration, blinds are pulled out over many shops – it must have been a sunny day. Another horse and cart proudly clip-clops along New Street. Far left, below, can be seen the Huddersfield Building Society, and the last photograph shows the bandstand in Greenhead Park, with Trinity Church in the distance. On the back of the photograph someone wrote to Miss Annie Lodge, of Whitehead Road, Primrose Hill: 'Hope you enjoyed yourself in the field last night. Should you go to Farnley, look out for a chap with a dog about 7.' I wonder if the tryst was kept?

ACKNOWLEDGEMENTS

My thanks to: Mrs Betty Swales (née Key), Mr and Mrs Roy Firth, Mrs Muriel Kelly, Mrs Lesley Parkinson, Mr Harold Taylor of Huddersfield Thespians Mr Jack Firth, and Mr and Mrs Gerald Hirst for kindly supplying photographs.

For identifying people, thanks to: Mr and Mrs Trevor Bray (Holmfirth Photographers) Mr John Babb, Mrs Marjorie Longstaff, Mr and Mrs Tom Jessop, Mrs Olive Charlesworth, Mr and Mrs Stanley Clay, Mrs Moon and Julie, Mrs Dorothy Southers and Mrs Genine Jackson.

Grateful thanks to Mrs Thelma Barlow, Greaves Photographers (Huddersfield), The *Huddersfield Examiner*, and staff of the Public Library Reference and Archives Department, for information relevant to photographs.

Finally, affectionate, posthumous acknowledgements to the late Miss Annie Whitworth, who left me her albums of old photographs. Also to my late parents, Hilda and Joe Taylor, for communicating their love of history, music and fascinating stories over the years.

Old Photographs can truly be everybody's best friends – to live in them is never to die.